A VISUAL FEAST

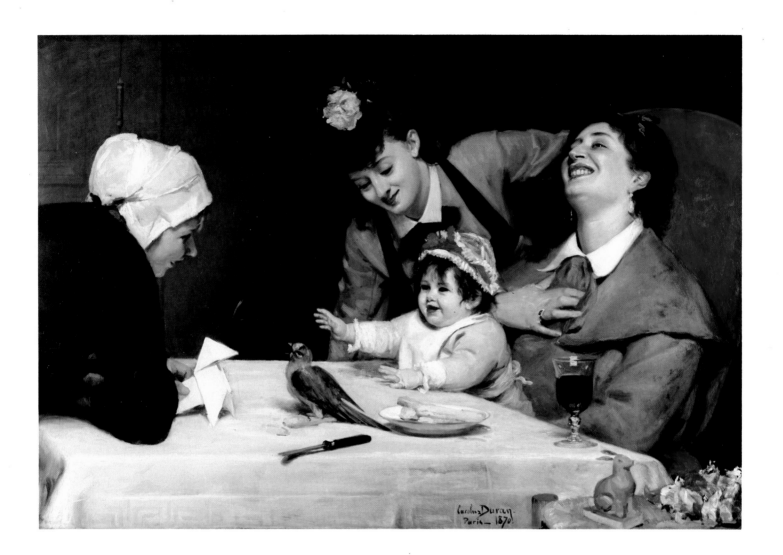

A VISUAL FEAST

Founders Society Detroit Institute of Arts

Edited by Cynthia Jo Fogliatti

The Detroit Institute of Arts Cookbook

The Detroit Institute of Arts
5200 Woodward Avenue
Detroit, Michigan 48202

Printed in the United States of America
89 88 87 86 85 5 4 3 2 1

Library of Congress Cataloging in Publication Data

A Visual feast.

    Includes index.
    1. Cookery.   I. Detroit Institute of Arts.
TX715.V685 1985   641.5   85-25331
ISBN 0-89558-114-0

Designers: Marc Alain Meadows and Robert Wiser, Meadows & Wiser, Washington, D.C.

Photographers: Dirk Bakker, Chief Museum Photographer, and Robert Hensleigh,
Associate Museum Photographer, The Detroit Institute of Arts

Typeset in Galliard by General Typographers, Inc., Washington, D.C.
8,000 copies printed on 80-pound Warren LOE Dull by Wolk Press, Inc., Woodlawn, Md.

Front Cover: Pieter Bruegel the Elder, Flemish, 1525/30-1569, *The Wedding Dance,* 1566,
oil on oak panel, 119.3 x 157.5 cm. City of Detroit Purchase (30.374).

Endleaves: Turkish (Bursa), *Summer Carpet,* Ottoman Dynasty, early 16th cent., cut and
voided velvet, satin, and silver thread, l. 490.2 x w. 268 cm. Gift of Mr. and Mrs. Eugene H.
Welker (48.137).

Frontispiece: Carolus-Duran (Charles-Emile-Auguste Durand), French, 1837-1917,
Merrymakers, 1870, oil on canvas, 90.2 x 139.7 cm. Founders Society Purchase, Robert H.
Tannahill Foundation Fund (80.37).

Back Cover: Anonymous Flemish or German Artist, *Still Life with Strawberries,*
ca. 1600/25, 27.9 x 41.6 cm. Gift of Mrs. Anna Scripps Whitcomb (35.106).

CONTENTS

William Adolphe Bouguereau, French,
1825-1905, *Bacchante*, 1894, oil on canvas,
152.4 x 88.9 cm. Gift of Dr. and Mrs. Edwin
S. Smyd (77.65).

PREFACE

Welcome to *A Visual Feast: The Detroit Institute of Arts Cookbook*, a publication that represents the culmination of three years of spirit and energy, labor and love devoted to the support of the Detroit Institute of Arts. This project began with an appeal to the museum's staff members, volunteers, and friends to share their secrets for nourishing the senses. The response from Detroit's "kitchen artists" was overwhelming; without the support of all those who contributed — not only recipes but their encouragement, expertise, and patience — a project of this scope would not have been possible.

We regret that limited space did not permit the use of all of the wonderful recipes submitted. The testing and selection of recipes was much more difficult than anticipated. Many thanks are due to all of the dedicated testers who extended their unflagging enthusiasm and cooperation, volunteered their kitchens, and loosened their belts!

We are very pleased to present to you *A Visual Feast* — a compendium of recipes as varied as the people of our state and as rich as the art works in the collection of the Detroit Institute of Arts. We invite you to enjoy to the fullest both the visual and the palatable treasures contained in this book, and thank you for your support of the museum.

The Cookbook Committee _____

Jane Solomon and Margie Gillis, Co-Chairs

Joy Emery, Vice-Chair

Charlotte Rosenthal and Trudy Wineman, Testing Committee

Vivian Berry	*Ruth Holcomb*	*Vi Reghanti*
Doris Burton	*Mary Ellen Johnson*	*George Russel*
Gayle Camden	*Virginia Johnston*	*Shirley Stanford*
Sue Clippert	*Lucie Kelly*	*Lois Stulberg*
Marilyn Farber	*Margot Kessler*	*Eleanor Sugarman*
Carole Frank	*Judi Layton*	*Joyce Tuck*
Frances Goldberg	*Kaia Lohmann*	*Nettie Weinberg*
Gay Healy	*Jan Miller*	*Connie Wineman*
Kay Hoff	*Harriet Prentis*	

INTRODUCTION

A Visual Feast: The Detroit Institute of Arts Cookbook, published as part of the museum's centennial celebration program, appropriately blends culinary and artistic interests. Food has been depicted in abundant variety by artists of every period and culture, from seventeenth-century still lifes, such as Dutch artist Abraham Hendricksz. van Beyeren's *Preparations for a Meal*, to whimsical twentieth-century Pop Art sculptures, such as American artist Claes Oldenburg's *Alphabet/Good Humor*, and including functional objects in many styles used to display or serve food.

This cookbook, a first for the Detroit Institute of Arts, features a fine collection of recipes gathered from the museum's staff, volunteers, and friends, and includes selected recipes from the museum's popular winter holiday *Wassail Feast*. The recipes range widely, from exotic African, Asian, and Indian dishes to hearty Celtic, German, and Polish fare, French delicacies, and savory Greek and Spanish dishes, thus emphasizing the rich, ethnic heritage of Detroit. Also to be found are recipes utilizing Michigan's bountiful wild game, succulent blueberries, strawberries, and peaches, sweet maple syrup, and excellent salmon.

Works of art from the museum's diverse collections, many of which depict food or are associated with the preparation, serving, or enjoyment of such, have been chosen to complement the recipes. *Summer,* by Alexandre François Desportes, depicts fully ripened fruits and vegetables arranged in baskets and framed by colorful blossoms. Similarly, a fresh array of seafood is the subject of William Merritt Chase's *The Yield of the Waters*. Objects of everyday use include the Greek *Column Krater*, a vessel for mixing wine and water, the English *Punch Pot*, and the African *Lidded Bowl with Lioness*. In *The Country Lunch*, by Jean François de Troy, the association of food with good company during a leisurely afternoon evokes great pleasure while *Café*, by Ernst Ludwig Kirchner, depicts the relaxed attitude of coffee drinkers.

It is our hope that these works, and the others featured here, will serve as an introduction to the Detroit Institute of Arts' collections, and that the recipes they accompany will delight and please a variety of palates. As the centennial program of the Detroit Institute of Arts continues, what better way to celebrate than with *A Visual Feast*!

Samuel Sachs II   *Director, The Detroit Institute of Arts*

American, *Side Chair* (one of a pair), 1760/90, mahogany, 101.6 x 59.7 x 54.6 cm. Founders Society Purchase, Beatrice Rogers Bequest Fund and contributions from Mr. and Mrs. Alvan Macauley, Jr., Mr. and Mrs. George F. Green, Dr. and Mrs. Irving Levitt, Mr. and Mrs. Irving J. Minett, Mr. and Mrs. Philip Caldwell, Mr. and Mrs. James O. Keene, Dr. and Mrs. John Kretzschmar, Mr. and Mrs. Richard Manoogian, and Edward Rothman in honor of Robert H. Tannahill (69.57).

ACKNOWLEDGMENTS

We would like to extend our gratitude to the following individuals and organizations for their generous support of *A Visual Feast: The Detroit Institute of Arts Cookbook*:

Lynn W. Day

Founders Junior Council

Margaret Gillis

Nathaniel and Mildred Gold

Independence Health Plan
   of Southeastern Michigan

Katherine Macauley

Lois Proctor Mack

Edna Minkin

Jane and Jack Solomon

Stroh Foundation

Elizabeth Webber Tost

Walter & Josephine Ford Fund

Women's Committee

Space will not allow the individual acknowledgment of all those who contributed to the realization of this book, but great appreciation goes to each staff member, volunteer, or friend of the museum for the encouragement given this project and the willingness to share prized recipes. Thanks are also due to Marc Alain Meadows for his sensitivity to the particular problems of design encountered in a project of this nature.

APPETIZERS
AND FIRST COURSES

*T*he custom of serving appetizers — food intended to stimulate the appetite — is nearly universal. Although the origin of the practice is not known, almost every country's cuisine includes recipes designed to prime the tastebuds for the feast to follow. Whether French-inspired hors d'oeuvres and classic canapés served on an elegant silver *Salver,* delicious dips presented in an unusual *Lidded Bowl with Lioness,* or slightly more substantial fare, the appetizer or first course is firmly established in American dining and entertaining traditions.

Included here are a variety of tantalizing treats ideal for cocktail parties or buffets, as stage-setters for elaborate meals, or perhaps as light snacks to be served with tea or coffee in an intimate setting such as that in *The Tea Table,* by Henri Le Sidaner.

In the broader sense a French Impressionist, Le Sidaner was, more specifically, an Intimist, or painter of scenes in which he narrowed the focus in order to heighten the sense of intimacy and close personal involvement of the viewer with the subject. The peaceful, sun-dappled courtyard depicted here suggests the perfect setting for sipping, nibbling, and discussing the many parallels between fine food and fine art.

Henri Eugène Augustin Le Sidaner, French, 1862–1939, *The Tea Table* (detail), 1919, oil on canvas, 72.4 x 91.4 cm. City of Detroit Purchase (21.73).

Beoreg

Delicious meat-filled pastries redolent of the spices of the East —

1 cup plus 2 tablespoons butter or margarine
3 pounds leg of lamb, ground
6 medium onions, minced
1/2–1 teaspoon allspice
Salt and pepper to taste
1/4 pound pine nuts, browned in butter
1 pound phylo dough

In a large frying pan, melt 2 tablespoons of the butter, add the ground lamb, and cook over medium heat until no pink remains. Add the chopped onions and cook until translucent. Add the allspice, salt, and pepper to taste and cook a few minutes longer. Add the pine nuts, heat through, and set aside. Melt the remaining butter in a small saucepan. Unfold the phylo dough, cut into 6 lengthwise strips, and cover with a damp towel. Working with one strip at a time, brush with the melted butter, place one heaping teaspoon of the filling in the lower left-hand corner of the dough, and fold over to make a triangle at the bottom of the strip. Continue folding the dough in triangles until the top of the strip is reached. Use melted butter to seal the final fold.* Place the finished triangles on a cookie sheet and bake in a 375°F. oven for 15–20 minutes or until lightly browned.

*The pastries may be frozen at this point for later baking.
   Yields 100

Jeanette Keramedjian

Bleu Cheese Balls

These tangy timesavers are certain to please.

1 10-ounce can buttermilk biscuits
1/2 cup butter
Bleu cheese to taste

Preheat the oven to 450°F. In a saucepan, melt the butter and keep warm. Cut each biscuit into quarters and roll into balls. Place the balls in an 8-inch square or round baking pan, taking care not to let them touch the sides of the pan. Pour one-half of the melted butter over the biscuits and bake for 4 minutes or until the balls begin to rise. Remove from the oven, cover with the remaining melted butter, and crumble bleu cheese over the top. Continue baking until browned.
   Serves 10–12

Andrew L. Camden

Jarlsberg Puff

The tangy flavors of Jarlsberg and Alouette fill this golden pastry pillow.

1 12- by 18-inch sheet puff pastry
1 pound Jarlsberg cheese, rind removed and cut into a rectangle
Dijon mustard
4 1/2 ounces Alouette cheese
1 egg white, beaten

Preheat the oven to 350° F. Spread the pastry on a cookie sheet, place the Jarlsberg cheese in the center, and coat with mustard. Spread a layer of Alouette cheese on top of the mustard and fold the pastry around the filling. Seal the opening with wet fingers and brush the pastry with the egg white. Bake for approximately 1 hour or until lightly browned (cover the top with foil if the pastry begins to brown too quickly). Serve immediately.
   Serves 10–12

Reva Moss

African (Barotse), *Lidded Bowl with Lioness,* late 19th cent., wood, 44.4 x 21.6 x 18.4 cm. Founders Society Purchase, African Art Gallery Committee Fund (82.50.1–.2).

Banker's Dip

As rich as its name —

1 cup mayonnaise
3 teaspoons soy sauce
1 teaspoon white vinegar
1 teaspoon curry powder
3 teaspoons onion, chopped

Combine all of the ingredients, blend well, and chill. Serve with fresh vegetables or shrimp.
Yields 1½ cups

Betty Bird

Feta Pastries

Inspired delights from the Grecian Isles —

¼ pound feta cheese, crumbled and sieved
¼ pound ricotta cheese, crumbled and
    sieved
¼ cup yogurt
1 egg
2 tablespoons fresh parsley, minced
5 leaves phylo dough
Butter, melted

Combine the cheeses, yogurt, egg, and parsley and set aside. Keep the phylo leaves covered with plastic wrap or a damp towel. Working with one leaf at a time, brush with melted butter, fold in half crosswise to form a rectangle, and brush again. Spread a narrow strip of the cheese mixture (about ¼ cup) along the folded edge of the dough, leaving a ½-inch border on each side of the filling. Fold in the sides of the leaf, roll up as if for a jelly roll,* brush the outside with butter, and place on a greased baking sheet. Repeat this process to make 4 more rolls. Bake at 400°F. for 20 minutes, cool, and cut each roll diagonally into six 2-inch lengths.
At this point the pastries may be frozen for later baking.
Yields 30

Mary Ann Simon

Baked Brie with Almonds

A spectacular offering needing minimal preparation —

2 pounds Brie cheese, chilled
2¼ ounces slivered almonds, toasted
French bread, sliced thinly, or melba
    rounds

Preheat the oven to 350°F. Remove the rind only from the top of the cheese. Place the Brie on the bottom of a 9-inch springform pan or quiche dish and put the dish on a baking sheet. Bake for 5–10 minutes or until the Brie begins to melt, remove from the oven, and sprinkle with the almonds. Place under the broiler, approximately 6 inches from the heating element, and broil until the almonds are lightly browned. Serve immediately with French bread or melba rounds.
Serves 12

Andrea Bailey

Japanese, *Wine Flask (Heishi)*, Muromachi Period, 1392–1573, lacquer, black negro ware with red painted decoration, h. 35 cm. Founders Society Purchase, Stoddard Fund for Asian Art and funds from the Gerald W. Chamberlin Foundation, Inc. (80.27).

Green Chili Won Tons

East meets Southwest in this zesty canapé.

1 pound Monterey Jack cheese, grated
2/3 cup canned green chilies, drained and chopped
1/3 cup canned jalapeño peppers, drained and chopped
Won ton wrappers
Peanut oil
Guacamole Dipping Sauce
(recipe follows)

Combine the cheese, chilies, and peppers, mix well, and place 1 teaspoon of filling in the center of each won ton wrapper. Completely cover the filling by first folding the bottom corner of the wrappers up, the side corners in, and the top corner down (moisten the top corner with water to seal).* Heat the peanut oil to 360°F. in a deep fryer or wok and fry 6–8 won tons at a time until golden. Transfer the won tons with a slotted spoon to paper towels to drain. Serve hot with *Guacamole Dipping Sauce.*

*At this point the won tons may be frozen for up to one month.
Yields 40–50

Guacamole Dipping Sauce

2 ripe avocados, mashed
1/2 cup green onions, chopped
3 tablespoons fresh lemon or lime juice
1 tablespoon mayonnaise
1/2 teaspoon coriander
Salt and pepper to taste

In a bowl, thoroughly combine all of the ingredients and cover with foil.* Serve with *Green Chili Won Tons.*
*Leave the avocado pits in the bowl or sprinkle with lemon or lime juice to help prevent darkening.

Yields approximately 1 cup

Joy Emery

Pâté Mousse au Beurre

A tempting terrine for any party table —

1/2 pound butter, divided into tablespoons and softened
1/3 cup red onions, chopped, rinsed in cold water, and drained
1/4 cup tart apples, peeled and chopped
2 tablespoons shallots, chopped
1 pound chicken livers, halved
1/4 cup brandy
1 teaspoon lemon juice
3 tablespoons heavy cream
1 teaspoon salt
1/4 teaspoon freshly ground black pepper
1/2 pound butter, clarified

In a skillet, melt 3 tablespoons of the softened butter, add the onions, and sauté for 5 minutes. Add the apples and shallots and cook 2 minutes more. Place the mixture in a food processor or blender and process thoroughly. In the same skillet, melt 3 more tablespoons of the butter and brown the chicken livers for 3–4 minutes over high heat. Add the brandy and cook for 2 minutes more. Add the livers and lemon juice to the apple and onion mixture in the food processor and blend. Add the cream and blend just until smooth. Transfer the

mixture to a bowl and let stand to cool.

Add the remaining softened butter, lemon juice, salt, and pepper to the pâté mixture, blend thoroughly, and ladle into a terrine or other container. Pour clarified butter over the top, covering completely, to form a seal about 1/8-inch thick. Chill for 2 hours or more before serving.

Yields 1 quart

Andrew L. Camden

African (Kongo [Zaire]), *Knife Case*, 16th-18th cent., ivory, 32.4 x 11.1 cm. City of Detroit Purchase (25.183).

Game Pâté

The hunter's reward, always in season —

12 ounces game (such as woodcock,
    pheasant, partridge, quail, or wild
    duck), boned
2 tablespoons brandy
1–2 game or chicken livers (optional)
8 ounces pork fat
1 small-medium onion, minced
1 tablespoon butter
1 cup port or Madeira
12 ounces lean pork, minced
12 ounces lean veal, minced
1 egg, beaten slightly
½ teaspoon salt
Black pepper to taste
½ teaspoon allspice (optional)
6–8 juniper berries, crushed
1 clove garlic
Salt pork or fat bacon, blanched
Bay leaves
Pine nuts or pistachios (optional)

Cut a few strips from the breast of the bird and marinate in brandy for 1 hour or more. Mince the remaining game and liver with a knife or in a food processor and set aside. Cut a small portion of the pork fat into decorative strips and reserve; chop the remaining fat into small cubes and set aside.

Sauté the onion briefly in the butter, then add the brandy (but not the marinated game strips), minced game and livers, pork fat cubes, wine, pork, veal, beaten egg, salt, pepper, allspice, juniper berries, and garlic. Blend the ingredients thoroughly and let stand for 1 hour or more.

Line a terrine with the blanched salt pork or bacon and fill with one-half of the pâté, packing the mixture in firmly. Cover the pâté with the marinated game strips, top with the remaining pâté, and decorate in a criss-cross pattern of pork fat strips and bay leaves. Cover the terrine with foil and a lid, set in a pan of hot water, and bake at 350°F. for approximately 1½ hours (pâté is done when it shrinks from the sides of the terrine). Let the pâté stand to cool before refrigerating. Serve chilled with a tangy sauce, such as *Cumberland Sauce* (see recipe p. 120), on the side.
    Serves 12

Jean W. Hudson

Pecans

Sweetmeats that whet the appetite —

Vegetable cooking spray
2 egg whites
2 tablespoons cold water
1½ cups sugar
2 teaspoons cinnamon
2 teaspoons salt
3 pounds pecans

Preheat the oven to 425°F. Spray a cookie sheet with a light coating of vegetable spray and set aside. Beat the egg whites with the water until frothy but not stiff. In a separate bowl, combine the sugar, cinnamon, and salt. Dip the pecans in the egg whites, then in the sugar and cinnamon mixture, and again in the egg whites. Spread the nuts in one layer on the cookie sheet and bake for 1 hour (turn every 10 minutes in the last ½ hour of baking time).
    Yields 3 pounds

Selma Winston

On page 15 of the Appetizers, oven temp. should be 275° and not 425° (PECANS)

Lettuce Packets with Spicy Peanut Sauce

An African-inspired variation on the Oriental spring roll —

2 heads Boston or iceberg lettuce
8 dried black mushrooms
Boiling water
16 fresh water chestnuts, diced
¾ pound pork or chicken, ground coarsely
1 egg, beaten lightly
1½ tablespoons dark soy sauce
½ teaspoon natural meat tenderizer
  (optional)
4 teaspoons cornstarch
2 tablespoons dry sherry
½ cup chicken broth
1 teaspoon sugar
1 teaspoon salt
4 tablespoons peanut oil

3–6 small, hot, dried red peppers (or to
  taste)
1 cup celery, diced
Spicy Peanut Sauce
  (recipe follows)

Carefully peel away 20–24 large lettuce leaves and set aside. Cover the mushrooms with boiling water, let stand 15 minutes, and drain, squeezing the water from the mushrooms (the liquid may be saved and used to flavor stock). Finely chop the mushrooms, combine with the water chestnuts, and set aside. Combine the pork, egg, soy sauce, meat tenderizer, and 3 teaspons of the cornstarch, mix well, and set aside. Combine the sherry, ¼ cup of the chicken broth, sugar, and salt and set aside. Blend together the remaining cornstarch and chicken broth and set aside.

In a wok over moderately high heat, heat the peanut oil until hot but not smoking. Add the peppers and stir fry for 15 seconds. Add the port mixture, stir to separate, and when the meat is no longer pink, add the mushroom mixture. Cook about 15 seconds more, stir in the cornstarch mixture, then add the celery and cook until heated through.

To serve, mound the meat mixture on a warm platter and serve accompanied by the lettuce leaves and a small bowl of *Spicy Peanut Sauce*. Guests should help themselves to a leaf, place a spoonful of the meat mixture and a small spoonful of sauce in the center, tuck and wrap the leaf around the filling, and eat with the fingers.

Serves 8–12 as an appetizer (or 4 as an entrée)

Spicy Peanut Sauce

1 cup chunky peanut butter
1 tablespoon fresh ginger, shredded
1 tablespoon spicy chutney
Juice of ½ lemon
Rind of ½ lemon, minced

In a blender or food processor, combine all of the ingredients and process just enough to blend.
  Yields 1 cup

Joy Emery

Chinese, *Ewer*, Ming Dynasty, late 15th cent., porcelain with underglaze cobalt, h. 25.4 cm. Gift of the Honorable and Mrs. G. Mennen Williams (73.320).

Moore Hot Puffs

Guaranteed to attract a following —

⅓ cup Parmesan cheese
⅔ cup mayonnaise
½ cup onions, minced
Whole wheat or white bread rounds
  (cut 2–3 inches in diameter)

Combine the Parmesan, mayonnaise, and onions and blend well. Toast the bread rounds on one side, spread the untoasted sides with the cheese mixture, and place under the broiler briefly or until the cheese is browned and bubbly.
  Yields 2–3 dozen

Mary Moore Denison

Fillet of Sole en Bloc

This gourmet's delight is a delectable combination of fruits of the sea.

1 pound fillet of sole
1 pound fillet of pickerel
6 large onions, chopped
3 tablespooons butter
1 tablespoon vegetable oil
3 eggs
1 teaspoon sugar
3 tablespoons bread crumbs
Juice of ½ lemon
2 teaspoons salt
Pepper to taste
1 lemon, quartered
Watercress or parsley
Horseradish Sauce
    (recipe follows)

Preheat the oven to 350°F. Using a food processor or small food mill, grind together the sole and pickerel and set aside. Reserve 1 cup of the chopped onion and sauté the remaining in the butter and oil until golden. In a large bowl, beat the eggs, add the ground fish, fresh and cooked onion, sugar, bread crumbs, lemon juice, salt, and pepper, and combine thoroughly. Transfer the mixture to an oiled, 9- by 5-inch loaf pan or 2-quart baking dish and bake for 1 hour. Let the loaf stand until room temperature, then remove to the refrigerator and chill for at least 3 hours. Turn the pâté out onto a platter, garnish with lemon wedges, watercress, and/or parsley, and serve with *Horseradish Sauce*.

Serves 12 as a first course (or 6 as a luncheon dish)

Horseradish Sauce

2 tablespoons Wasabi powder* combined
    with a small amount of water
½ cup sour cream
½ cup mayonnaise
1½ tablespoons lemon juice
Dash of Tabasco sauce
Salt to taste
2 tablespoons horseradish (or to taste)

In a bowl, combine all of the ingredients, blend thoroughly, and chill in the refrigerator for several hours before serving.
    *Wasabi powder may be found at most Asian groceries or specialty food stores.
    Yields approximately 1 cup

Marilyn Farber

Salmon Michigan

Smooth salmon mousse served in a buttery, golden crust —

3 tablespoons butter, melted
1 cup cracker crumbs
2 tablespoons onion, grated
2 8-ounce packages cream cheese, cubed
¼ teaspoon salt
⅛ teaspoon pepper
2 teaspoons lemon juice
1½ cups sour cream
3 eggs
1 15½-ounce can red salmon, rinsed,
    drained, bones and skin removed
Parsley, chopped

Preheat the oven to 350°F. Grease an 8-inch springform pan, cut a piece of waxed paper to fit the bottom, and set aside. In a small saucepan, melt the butter, combine with the cracker crumbs, and press into the bottom of the pan. Bake the crust for 10 minutes, remove from the oven, and set aside. In a food processor, finely chop the onion, add the cream cheese, salt, pepper, lemon juice, and ¼ cup of the sour cream, and process until smooth. Add the eggs, process briefly, and fold in the salmon. Pour the mixture into the prepared pan, bake for 45–50 minutes or until set, remove from the oven, and run a knife around the edge of the pan to loosen. Transfer the pan to a rack to cool, remove the side of the pan, and spread the side of the cake with the remaining sour cream. Garnish with chopped parsley and serve.
    Serves 12

Connie Wineman

Turkish (Iznik), *Underglaze Painted Polychrome Plate*, Ottoman Dynasty, late 16th-early 17th cent., composite body with clear glaze, diam. 34.3 cm. City Appropriation (28.91).

Herbed Pork, Spinach, and Chicken Liver Terrine

A sumptuous spread with a hint of Madeira —

1½ pounds spinach, washed and trimmed
    (or 1½ 10-ounce packages frozen
    spinach)
2 quarts boiling water
1½ pounds pork shoulder, ground
¾ pound bacon, sliced
¼ pound bacon, minced
4 eggs, beaten lightly
⅓ cup flat-leaved parsley, minced
2 cloves garlic, minced
4 teaspoons basil, minced
1 tablespoon thyme
Salt, pepper, and nutmeg to taste
2 tablespoons unflavored gelatin
⅓ cup Madeira
3 tablespoons butter
1 cup scallions, chopped
½ pound chicken livers, trimmed and cut
    into ½-inch pieces
¼ cup cognac
⅓ cup heavy cream

In a saucepan, blanch the spinach in the boiling water for 3 minutes, drain, rinse under cold water, and dry well. Chop the spinach coarsely in a food processor, transfer to a large bowl, add the ground pork, minced bacon, beaten eggs, parsley, garlic, basil, thyme, salt, pepper, and nutmeg, and set aside. In a small bowl, sprinkle the gelatin over the Madeira and let stand 10 minutes to soften.

In a skillet, melt the butter and sauté the scallions over medium heat for 5 minutes. Add the chicken livers and sauté over moderately high heat until lightly browned outside but still pink inside. Add the livers and scallions to the pork mixture and set aside. Add the cognac to the pan, stir to deglaze, then stir in the cream and the gelatin mixture. Add the cognac to the pork mixture, combining well.

Line a 1½-quart terrine with the remaining bacon slices, letting the ends of the strips hang over the sides of the terrine. Fill the terrine with the pork mixture, packing well and mounding the mixture slightly in the center, and fold the bacon strips over the top. Cover with foil and a lid, place in a larger baking pan, and surround with hot water to one-half the depth of the terrine. Bake in a 350°F. oven for 2 hours, remove the terrine from the baking pan, and let stand for 15 minutes. Remove the lid and, leaving the foil intact, place a 4-pound weight on the top. Let stand at room temperature to cool and refrigerate overnight. Remove the weight and foil, run a thin knife around the inside edge of the terrine, and invert over a platter. Garnish with watercress, gherkins, or radishes and serve sliced with French bread.

Yields 1½ quarts

The Cookbook Committee

Red Caviar Roll

A brilliant red accent to the holiday buffet table —

¼ cup butter
½ cup flour, sifted
2 cups milk
4 eggs, separated
1 tablespoon lemon juice
4 ounces cream cheese
8 ounces red caviar
Parsley, chopped

Preheat the oven to 350°F. Grease a jelly roll pan, line with waxed paper, grease the paper, and set aside. In a saucepan, melt the butter, stir in the flour, and cook for 1 minute. Add the milk, bring to a simmer, stirring constantly, cook for 1 minute, and remove from the heat. Beat in the egg yolks one at a time and set aside. Beat the egg whites until stiff peaks form, fold into the egg yolk mixture, and blend thoroughly. Evenly spread the mixture over the greased paper in the jelly roll pan, bake for 50 minutes, test for doneness (the cake should be very lightly browned), and let stand to cool.

In a bowl, blend together the lemon juice and cream cheese, gently stir in the caviar, and set aside. Loosen the edges of the cake, turn onto waxed paper, and peel away the greased paper. Spread the cake with the caviar mixture and roll, using the waxed paper as an aid, as if for a jelly roll. Transfer the roll to the refrigerator to chill. Serve sprinkled with chopped parsley.

Serves 6–8

Jackie Eckhous

Samuel van Hoogstraten (or Follower), Dutch, 1627-1678, *Perspective Box of a Dutch Interior,* 17th cent., oil paint, glass mirror, and walnut, 42.2 x 30.5 x 28.3 cm. Founders Society Purchase, Membership and Donations Fund (35.101).

A. Sev'yer, Russian, active 1892–95, *Salver*, 1894, silver, diam. 52.7 cm. Gift of Raymond C. Smith (F79.95).

Shrimp Remoulade

Chilled seafood in a hot and zesty marinade —

1 5½-ounce jar Zatarhian Creole Mustard
½ cup vinegar
¾ cup oil
3 teaspoons paprika
6 green onions with tops, chopped
2 tablespoons fresh parsley, chopped
1 teaspoon lemon juice
Few dashes of Worcestershire sauce

20 drops of Tabasco sauce (or to taste)
1 pound or more shrimp, cooked and cleaned
Lettuce, shredded

In a large bowl, combine all of the ingredients except for the lettuce and marinate for 4 hours or overnight in the refrigerator. Approximately 30 minutes

before serving, cover the bottom of a large salad bowl or individual plates with the shredded lettuce, spoon the shrimp and marinade into the center, and serve with warm, crusty French bread.
    Serves 4

Charlotte Rosenthal

Oysters Rockefeller à la Winston

A new interpretation of an old favorite —

24 oysters (in shells)
2 10-ounce packages frozen, chopped
    spinach, thawed and drained
16 ounces sour cream
1 large clove garlic, crushed
1 tablespoon Pernod
Salt and pepper to taste
Parmesan cheese, grated
Butter

Preheat the broiler to 450–500°F. Clean and remove the oysters from the shells (reserve the bottom halves of the shells) and set aside. Purée the spinach in a food processor or blender, add the sour cream, garlic, and Pernod, generously add salt and pepper, and process to blend. Spread the spinach mixture in the bottom of the oyster shells, place the oysters on top, and cover with the remaining spinach mixture. Sprinkle

generously with the Parmesan, dot with butter, and place on a cookie sheet.* Place under the broiler for approximately 5 minutes or until the cheese is well browned. Serve immediately.
    *At this point the oysters may be frozen.
    Serves 8–12

Selma Winston

Salami Sausage

Perfect for hearty meals al fresco —

2 pounds lean ground beef
½ teaspoon mustard seed
½ teaspoon garlic powder
¼ teaspoon marjoram
3 tablespoons curing salt
¼ teaspoon sage

1 teaspoon sugar
1 cup water

Mix all of the ingredients thoroughly and divide into 3 portions. Roll each portion tightly in aluminum foil, tie the ends with string, and refrigerate for 3 days. Remove the sausages from the refrigerator, boil for 1 hour, let cool, and change the foil wrapping. Return the salami to the refrigerator to chill. Cut the sausages into thin slices before serving.
Yields 3 ½-pound sausages

James A. Bridenstine

Shad Roe Ring

A delicacy with flavor that never fails —

½ lemon, sliced
Water
2 7¾-ounce cans shad roe
1 envelope unflavored gelatin
1½ cups chicken broth
Watercress
1 cucumber, sliced

1 cup sour cream
1 teaspoon horseradish

Add the lemon slices to the water, poach the shad roe gently for 10 minutes, drain, and let cool. Remove the membranes, separate the eggs carefully, and pack the roe in an oiled, 8-inch ring mold. Dissolve the gelatin in the chicken broth, pour the mixture over the roe, and refrigerate until firm. Unmold and decorate with watercress and cucumber slices. Combine the sour cream and horseradish and serve on the side.
Serves 6

Mrs. Alger Shelden

Caviar Mousse

A royal spread fit for a tsar —

1 envelope unflavored gelatin
½ cup boiling water
½ cup cold water
6 eggs, hard-boiled
1 cup mayonnaise
2 tablespoons sour cream
1 teaspoon Dijon mustard
1 small onion, grated
Dash of Worcestershire sauce
Freshly ground pepper to taste
6 ounces red or black caviar, rinsed and
    drained
Sweet butter
Thin slices of dark bread

In a large pan, dissolve the gelatin in the boiling water, add the cold water, and mix in the eggs, mayonnaise, sour cream, mustard, onion, Worcestershire sauce, pepper, and caviar and blend thoroughly. Pour the mixture into a 3- to 4-cup mold and refrigerate overnight. Unmold the mousse onto a platter and serve with lightly buttered slices of dark bread.
Serves 12

Caryn R. Shaye

Turkish (Iznik), *Underglaze Painted Polychrome Plate,* Ottoman Dynasty, late 16th-early 17th cent., composite body with clear glaze, h. 6.4 x diam. 32.7 cm. City of Detroit Purchase (28.145).

Marinated Shrimp with Garlic Mushrooms and Artichoke Hearts

A piquant seafood-salad combination —

2 cups water
1 cup white wine
1 medium onion, chopped
1 stalk celery
1 tablespoon pickling spices
¼ teaspoon thyme
½ teaspoon tarragon
1 pound shrimp, cleaned and deveined
Garlic Mushrooms
    (see following recipe)

Conrad Bard and Robert Lamont,
American (in partnership 1841–45), *Pitcher
and Waiter*, 1841, silver, h. 42 cm (pitcher),
diam. 20.6 cm (waiter). Founders Society
Purchase, Beatrice W. Rogers Bequest Fund
(69.46–47).

Vinaigrette
    (see following recipe)
12 ounces artichoke hearts

In a large saucepan, combine the water,
wine, onion, celery, pickling spices,
thyme, and tarragon and bring to a boil.
Add the shrimp, return to a boil, and
cook for 1 minute. Remove the shrimp,
rinse in cold water, and transfer to a
bowl. Add the mushrooms and vinaigrette to the shrimp and marinate overnight in the refrigerator. Add the
artichoke hearts, marinate for 4–6 hours
more, drain, and serve.
    Serves 8

Garlic Mushrooms

1 clove garlic
1 teaspoon butter
1 pound mushroom caps
¼ cup white wine

In a skillet, sauté the garlic in the butter
until golden brown and remove from the
pan. Add the mushroom caps, sauté for 5

minutes, pour in the wine, cover, and
simmer for 5 minutes more. Remove the
pan from the heat and cool.
    Yields 1½–2 cups

Vinaigrette

3 tablespoons red wine vinegar
1 tablespoon lemon juice
½ teaspoon salt
½ teaspoon Dijon mustard
½ teaspoon sugar
½ teaspoon each dried basil, parsley, and
    chives (or the equivalent of fresh)
¾ cup olive oil

In a small bowl, combine all of the ingredients and stir briskly to blend.
    Yields approximately 1 cup

Irma E. Stevens

Quick Zucchini Custard Tart

This savory quiche is ideal as an hors d'oeuvre.

3 cups zucchini, sliced thinly
1 cup buttermilk baking mix
½ cup onion, minced
½ cup fresh Parmesan cheese, grated
2 tablespoons parsley, snipped
½ teaspoon seasoned salt
½ teaspoon oregano
Pepper to taste
1 clove garlic, minced
½ cup vegetable oil
4 eggs, beaten slightly

Combine all of the ingredients, blend
thoroughly, and spread in a greased, 9-
by 13-inch pan. Bake at 350°F. for approximately 40 minutes or until golden
brown. Let cool slightly, cut into small
squares, and serve.
    Yields 32–40

Marianne Letasi

African (Bembe), *Spoon,* early 20th cent., wood, 27.9 x 6 cm. Gift of Mr. and Mrs. Robert T Weston (1983.52).

Baba Ghanouj

An excellent eggplant dip that originated in Egypt —

3 medium eggplants
3 tablespoons tahini (sesame paste)
Juice of 1 lemon
2 tablespoons fresh oregano (or 2 teaspoons dried)
1 tablespoon fresh coriander (or 1 teaspoon dried)
2 cloves garlic, crushed
2 teaspoons salt
¼ cup olive oil
2 tablespoons sour cream
¼ cup yogurt
Hot red pepper sauce to taste
Lettuce leaves
Pita bread or crackers

Preheat the oven to 400°F. Prick the eggplants all over with a sharp fork, place on a cookie sheet, and bake until they collapse (about 45–50 minutes), turning two to three times. Remove the eggplants from the oven and let cool. In a food processor or blender, combine the tahini, lemon juice, oregano, coriander, garlic, and salt and process until smooth. Scrape the flesh of the cooled eggplants from the skins, add the flesh to the processor, and blend again until smooth. Add the olive oil, process until incorporated, then add the sour cream, yogurt, and hot pepper sauce, and process until well blended. Serve on lettuce leaves with pita bread and/or crackers.

Serves 15–20

Samuel Sachs II

Cheese Batons

A delicious surprise inside every golden crust —

12 very thin slices white bread, crusts trimmed
⅓ pound Gruyère cheese
Dijon mustard
Oil for deep frying

Soften the slices of bread by placing them between dampened paper towels for 30 minutes. In the meantime, slice the cheese into 12 strips approximately 3¼- by ⅓- by ⅓-inches. When the bread has softened, flatten between sheets of waxed paper using a rolling pin. Spread one side of each slice of bread with mustard, place a strip of cheese along one edge of each slice, and tightly roll the bread around the cheese strips. Wrap the batons tightly in small squares of aluminum foil and chill for 1 hour. Heat the oil to 375°F. Remove the foil, deep fry the batons in batches of 6 for 2–3 minutes or until golden brown, drain on paper towels, and serve.

Note: This recipe may be doubled easily.

Yields 12

Gayle Camden

SOUPS

*A*s long ago as the Middle Ages soups were a popular feature of every meal. It was not uncommon for a minimum of three to four soups to be served at one sitting in wealthy households, while at banquets more than a dozen varieties might be offered. Given the importance of these life-sustaining liquids, it is understandable that, from ancient times to the present, many vessels have been fashioned specifically to contain soups and utensils designed to serve them, such as the Etruscan *Ladle* fashioned of bronze in about 500 B.C. From the simple form and decoration of Chinese and Japanese bowls to the more ornate styles of the European Baroque and Rococo periods, few vessels could be as imaginative and colorful as this *Soup Tureen in the Form of a Turkey,* made in Strasbourg in 1755.

Nourishing and versatile, soups range from hearty meals-in-themselves to clear consommés and delicately flavored cream-based bisques. Our wide variety of soups, including a classic Italian minestrone, an aromatic French bouillabaisse, a spicy Creole gumbo, and a tart Russian borscht, will suit your every purpose or preference.

French (Strasbourg), *Soup Tureen in Form of a Turkey,* 1755, faience, 47.6 x 40.6 x 43.2 cm. Founders Society Purchase, Mrs. Edsel B. Ford Fund (65.25).

Cream of Curry Soup

A savory beginning for a special dinner —

2 cups chicken stock
1 cup heavy cream
½–1 teaspoon curry powder
1 tablespoon parsley, minced
2 eggs
½ cup sweet white wine or sauterne
Slivered almonds

In a saucepan, heat the chicken stock with the cream over medium to low heat. Add the curry powder and parsley, mix well, and remove from the heat just as the mixture comes to a boil. Beat the eggs lightly and stir in ½ cup of the hot stock. Gradually add the egg mixture to the remaining stock, whisking continuously. Add the wine, place the stock over medium to low heat, and whisk for 2 minutes more. Serve the soup topped with slivered almonds in warmed soup cups.

Serves 4

Mrs. Alger Shelden

Spring Carrot Soup

A creamy, vegetable delight —

3 tablespoons sweet butter
4 large shallots, minced
3 pounds (approximately 6 cups) small, tender carrots, chopped
1½–2 quarts chicken stock
Salt and white pepper to taste
3 tablespoons chervil, minced
½ cup heavy cream, whipped to soft peaks

Melt the butter over low heat and sauté the shallots for 5 minutes. Add the carrots, cook an additional 10 minutes, then add enough of the chicken stock to cover and cook until the carrots are just tender (about 25 minutes). Purée the soup in a food processor, blender, or food mill.* Return the mixture to the stove just long enough to heat through and season to taste with salt and pepper.

To serve, combine the chervil and the lightly whipped cream and float a large spoonful in each bowl of soup.

*The soup may be frozen at this point for later preparation.

Serves 8

Michael Fahlund

Scallion and Raw Mushroom Soup Dione

A rich, tangy taste experience —

¼ pound sweet butter
5 bunches scallions (with tops), minced
2 tablespoons flour
5 cups chicken stock
½ pound mushrooms, chopped
1¼ cups light cream
Salt and white pepper to taste
¼ pound mushrooms, sliced thinly
½ cup heavy cream, whipped
Dash of cayenne pepper

Beat the butter with a wooden spoon until it is light and fluffy. Add the scallions, mix thoroughly, and put in a heavy saucepan. Cover the pan and simmer for 10 minutes, being careful not to let the scallions take on color. Remove the pan from the heat and stir in the flour. When the mixture is smooth, add the chicken stock and blend well. Return the mixture to the heat and stir until it comes to a boil; reduce the heat and simmer for 10 minutes. Remove the pan from the heat and add the chopped mushrooms.

Put the soup through a blender or food processor in small batches and purée until smooth. Add the light cream to the soup and season to taste. Reheat the soup and add the finely sliced mushrooms. Serve at once with a large spoonful of whipped cream and a sprinkling of cayenne pepper in each bowl.

Serves 6

Joy Emery

Chinese, *Plate*, late Yüan/early Ming Dynasty, 14th cent., lacquer, diam. 29.2 cm. Founders Society Purchase, Stoddard Fund for Asian Art and the Gerald W. Chamberlin Foundation, Inc. (80.25).

Creamy Mushroom Soup

This versatile recipe is perfect for cold weather.

4 teaspoons chicken stock base
3 cups water
1 pound mushrooms, sliced *
2 8-ounce packages cream cheese, cubed
Salt and pepper to taste
Paprika to taste
Fresh parsley, chopped

Combine the chicken stock base and the water, add the mushrooms, and bring to a boil; reduce the heat and cook for 8–10 minutes. Place one-half of the cream cheese in a blender or food processor and process until smooth. Add one-half of the mushroom mixture, blend thoroughly, and transfer to a saucepan. Repeat with the remaining cream cheese and mushroom mixture and season to taste. Reheat the soup and serve in small cups with paprika and parsley sprinkled over the top as garnish.

The soup may be varied by substituting broccoli, cauliflower, carrots, or tomatoes for the mushrooms, and cooking the vegetables in the stock until tender.

Serves 6

Thayer Laurie

French Tomato Soup

Hearty eating à la française —

3 tablespoons butter
5 carrots, chopped
5 onions, chopped
4 cups canned plum tomatoes, chopped
  (reserve liquid)
½ teaspoon baking soda
¼ cup raw rice
2 quarts water
1 quart milk
½ cup cream

2 teaspoons chicken stock base
Salt and pepper to taste

Melt the butter in a large pot, add the carrots and onions, cover, and simmer for 15 minutes or until the vegetables are tender but not brown. Add the tomatoes with the reserved juice and the baking soda and continue to simmer. Wash the rice in running water, then cook in 2 quarts of rapidly boiling water until tender (about 10 minutes), and drain. Add the rice to the tomato mixture, then add the milk, cream, and chicken stock base. Blend well and simmer until very hot. Season the soup to taste and serve immediately.
  Serves 8–10

Mrs. Alvan Macauley, Jr.

Tomato Soup

This is a rich rendition of the classic recipe.

1 cup onion, chopped
½ cup butter, melted
2 tablespoons oil
1½ cups chicken stock
2 28-ounce cans tomatoes, mashed
2 tablespoons tomato paste
1 teaspoon sugar
½ teaspoon thyme

½ teaspoon basil
1 cup heavy cream
Croutons

Sauté the onion until soft in the melted butter and oil. Add the remaining ingredients except for the cream and croutons, mix thoroughly, and simmer for 30 minutes. Stir a little of the tomato mixture into the cream to blend and then whisk the cream into the remaining tomato mixture. Do not allow the soup to boil. Serve in large bowls topped with the croutons.
  Serves 6–8

Lucy Van Dusen

Cold Cantaloupe Soup

A delicate introduction to any meal —

1 large, ripe cantaloupe, peeled, seeded,
  and chopped
Juice of 1 lime
½ cup sugar
1 cup heavy cream
¼ teaspoon nutmeg
Rind of 1 lime, grated
Lime twists
Mint leaves

Place the chopped cantaloupe in a food processor or blender, add the lime juice and ¼ cup of the sugar, and blend at high speed until smooth; set aside. In a large bowl, beat together the cream, remaining sugar, and nutmeg until very thick. Fold the cream into the cantaloupe mixture and add the grated lime rind, stirring just until blended (do not overmix or the cream will separate from the cantaloupe). Pour the soup into a glass bowl and chill before serving. Garnish with lime twists and mint leaves.
  Serves 4

Ruth Glancy

Jimmy Schmidt's Raszolnik

Of Russian origin, this recipe owes its tanginess to an unusual blend of ingredients — pickles, buttermilk, and cream.

9 tablespoons butter
½ cup flour
1 quart chicken stock
1 cucumber, peeled, seeded, and halved
1 small onion, diced
1 small potato, peeled and diced
Water, salted
1½ dill pickles, peeled, seeded, and chopped
¼ cup dill pickle juice
2–3 cups buttermilk
1 cup cream (approximately)
Salt to taste
¼ teaspoon black pepper
1 tablespoon white wine vinegar (optional)
1 teaspoon fresh dill weed

In a large, heavy soup kettle, melt all but 1 tablespoon of the butter, add the flour, and stir until the mixture is bubbly. Stir in the chicken stock and cook, stirring constantly, until the mixture has thickened. Lower the heat and simmer for approximately 45 minutes. Purée one-half of the cucumber, dice the other, and set both aside. In a small saucepan, melt the remaining tablespoon of butter, add the onion, and cook until soft (approximately 5 minutes); set aside.

In another small saucepan, blanch the potato in lightly salted water for about 5 minutes or until only slightly firm, drain, and set aside. Add the puréed cucumber to the chicken stock mixture and cook an additional 15 minutes. Remove the mixture from the heat and add the diced cucumber, onion, potato, and chopped dill pickles. Cool the mixture to room temperature and refrigerate overnight.

To the chilled cucumber mixture, add the pickle juice and enough buttermilk and cream to reach desired consistency. Season with salt and pepper. If the tart pickle flavor is too weak, add a little white wine vinegar to the soup. Garnish with dill weed and serve chilled.
Serves 8–10

Cleo Gruber

Gazpacho

The dish to serve when the temperatures soar —

2 cloves garlic
2 tablespoons red wine vinegar
3 tablespoons olive oil
1 cup white bread (without crusts), torn into pieces
1½ pounds tomatoes, peeled, seeded, and diced
1 green pepper, diced
1 sweet red pepper, diced
1 cucumber, peeled, seeded, and diced
⅓ cup radishes, diced
¼ cup red onion, diced
⅓ cup celery heart, diced
¼ cup pitted black olives, diced
1 small hot pepper, seeded and minced
2 tablespoons fresh parsley, minced
2 cups tomato juice
½ cup ice water (approximately)
Garlic croutons
Yogurt (optional)
Coriander leaves, chopped (optional)
Dill (optional)

In a food processor, purée the garlic, vinegar, oil, and bread and transfer to a large bowl. Add the diced vegetables, black olives, hot pepper, parsley, and tomato juice and chill several hours or overnight. Stir in enough ice water to thin the soup to desired consistency. Correct the seasonings and serve with garlic croutons. A dollop of yogurt may be added to the soup along with coriander leaves or dill as a garnish.
Serves 6

Lydie A. Hudson

Arthur Stone, American, 1847–1938, *Pepper Caster*, 1906/07, sterling silver, parcel-gilt, h. 14.2 cm. Gift of Mr. and Mrs. James A. Beresford (76.169).

Potato Soup

This thick, rich rendition is flavored with bacon, leeks, and chervil.

4 slices lean bacon, diced
6 leeks (white portion only), sliced thinly
1/4 cup onion, chopped
2 tablespoons flour
4 cups beef broth
3 large potatoes, peeled and sliced thinly
2 egg yolks, beaten slightly
1 cup sour cream
1 tablespoon parsley, minced
1 tablespoon chervil, minced

In a 5-quart pot, sauté the bacon until it is almost crisp. Add the leeks and onion and sauté for an additional 5 minutes. Stir in the flour and add the broth in a slow stream while stirring constantly. Add the potatoes and simmer for 1 hour.* Combine the egg yolks and the sour cream, stir the mixture slowly into the soup, and simmer for 10 minutes, stirring constantly. Serve garnished with the parsley and chervil.

At this point, the soup may be frozen and stored for later preparation.
Serves 6

Judith Weston

Peanut Soup

An unusual, bold flavor from the South —

1 large onion, chopped
1 tablespoon butter
3 cups chicken broth
1 large tomato, peeled and chopped
1/2 cup tomato paste
1/4 teaspoon cayenne pepper
1/2–1 cup hot water

1/2 cup creamy peanut butter
Salt to taste

In a large kettle, sauté the onion in the butter until tender. Add the chicken broth, tomato, tomato paste, and cayenne pepper, cover, and simmer for 15 minutes. Blend together the hot water and the peanut butter until smooth, add to the soup, cover, and simmer for an additional 15 minutes. Add salt to taste and serve in small cups.
Serves 4–6

Jane Manoogian

London Chop House Pea Pod Soup

By special request, a dining favorite —

7 tablespoons butter
3/4 cup onion, chopped
3/4 cup leeks (white portion only), sliced
3 tablespoons flour
1 quart chicken broth
1 teaspoon sugar
1 bay leaf
1/2 teaspoon white pepper
1/2 teaspoon freshly ground nutmeg
Salt to taste
1 12-ounce package frozen peas
1 cup fresh Chinese pea pods, trimmed
    and cut into 1/4-inch pieces
2 egg yolks
1 cup heavy cream

Melt 6 tablespoons of the butter in a 3-quart saucepan, add the onions and leeks, and sauté until transparent. Add the flour, stir 1 minute, then add the chicken broth and stir until well blended. Add the sugar, bay leaf, pepper, and nutmeg, season to taste with salt, bring to a boil, and simmer for 15 minutes. Add the frozen peas, bring to a boil, and cook an additional 2–3 minutes.

Purée the mixture in a blender or food processor and strain through a fine sieve. Return the mixture to the saucepan and reheat. Sauté the pea pods in the remaining tablespoon of butter until they begin to take on color (but do not overcook) and add to the soup. Using a fork, beat the egg yolks with the cream and add gradually to the soup. Correct the seasonings to taste and serve.
Serves 6

Cleo Gruber

Vincent van Gogh, Dutch, 1853-1890, *The Diggers*, 1889, oil on canvas, 65.1 x 50.2 cm. Bequest of Robert H. Tannahill (70.158).

Cream of Artichoke Soup

A creamy concoction with artichokes at the heart —

1/2 cup green onions, chopped
1 stalk celery, chopped
1 medium carrot, chopped
1 bay leaf
1/8 teaspoon thyme
4 tablespoons butter
1 quart chicken broth
10 ounces fresh or frozen artichoke hearts, cooked and chopped
2 egg yolks, beaten lightly
1 cup heavy cream
Salt and pepper to taste

In a 2-quart saucepan, sauté the onions, celery, carrot, bay leaf, and thyme in the butter for 3-5 minutes. Add the chicken broth and simmer for 10 minutes. Add the artichoke hearts, simmer for another 5-10 minutes, and remove from the heat. Combine the egg yolks and the cream, add to the soup, and reheat, but do not allow the soup to come to a boil. Season with salt and pepper and serve.

Note: This rich, creamy soup is just as flavorful when made in advance and reheated for serving.

Serves 6

Mrs. Barry Holmes

African (Kuba [Zaire]), *Beaker in Form of Two Heads*, n.d.a., wood, 14.9 x 16.2 x diam. 6 cm. Bequest of Robert H. Tannahill (70.31).

Borscht

Authentically Russian, robust, and mouthwatering —

1 cup Great Northern beans
3 cups water
2 quarts Beef Stock, with meat (recipe follows)
4 large beets, peeled and diced
2 large potatoes, peeled and diced
1/2 head each green and red cabbage
6 tablespoons cider vinegar
2 tablespoons tomato paste
2 teaspoons salt
Pepper to taste
Sour cream

Soak the beans in the water overnight. Put the stock in a large pot and add the soaked beans along with any remaining liquid. Cover the pot and cook about 1 hour or until the beans are just tender. Add the remaining ingredients except for the sour cream, cover the pot, and cook until the vegetables are tender (approximately 30 minutes). Taste and adjust the seasonings: the flavor of the soup should be slightly tart. Add the diced meat and reheat. Serve in large bowls with a garnish of sour cream.

Serves 8-10

Beef Stock

4-5 pounds beef with bone (such as short ribs, shanks, or pot roast)
Vegetable oil
3 quarts water (approximately)
1 large onion, left unpeeled and chopped
2 carrots, peeled and chopped
1 stalk celery (with leaves), chopped
Few sprigs parsley

In a large pot, brown the meat in a small amount of oil, add water to cover, and bring to a boil. Skim the surface of the stock. Add the remaining ingredients, partially cover the pot, and simmer the stock for 2 hours or until the meat is tender. Remove the meat from the pot, cool, and dice; strain the stock. Cover the meat and the stock separately and store in the refrigerator overnight. When chilled thoroughly, skim the fat from the top.

Yields approximately 2 quarts

The Cookbook Committee

Waterzooi Soup

This hearty soup/stew is a favorite in Belgium.

1 onion
4 large leeks (white portion only)
3 large carrots
3 tablespoons butter
8 cups chicken stock
Bouquet Garni (or parsley, thyme, and bay leaf tied together)
4 pounds meaty chicken pieces
Juice of ½ lemon
¾ cup heavy cream
1 large stalk celery
3 egg yolks, beaten
Wondra Flour (optional)
Salt and pepper to taste
6 small potatoes, boiled and peeled
Parsley, chopped

Coarsely chop 1 onion, 1 leek, and 1 carrot. Place the vegetables in a large kettle with the butter, cover, and sauté for 5 minutes. Add the chicken stock and the Bouquet Garni, cover, and simmer for 30 minutes. Add the chicken pieces and simmer for 1 hour more. Remove the chicken and let cool. Strain the stock into another pot and boil until it is reduced by one-third.

Add the lemon juice to the cream and let sit until room temperature. Cut the remaining leeks, carrots, and celery into julienne strips, cook in boiling water until barely tender, and drain. Remove the cooked chicken from the bones, discard the skin and bones, and cut the meat into bite-sized pieces.

Add the beaten egg yolks to the soup and whisk until the soup has thickened;* add salt and pepper to taste. Add the chicken and vegetables to the soup and heat through. Serve in large, deep bowls with a boiled potato in each and garnished with a generous topping of chopped parsley.

For a thicker soup, shake Wondra Flour over the top and whisk until well blended.

Serves 6

Gaylord W. Gillis

Peasant Soup with Eggplant and Sausage

A hearty winter meal in itself—

1 quart water
⅓ cup dry white beans
1 cup onions, sliced thinly
1 cup leeks, sliced thinly
3 tablespoons butter
2 bay leaves
½ teaspoon sage
½ teaspoon thyme
Pepper to taste
1 pound eggplant, peeled and cut into ½-inch cubes
Dash of salt
2 tablespoons oil
3–4 cloves garlic, mashed
1 pound fresh or canned tomatoes, peeled, seeded, and chopped (drain and reserve liquid)
¾ pound pre-cooked sweet Italian or Polish sausage
2 tablespoons basil
2 tablespoons chives
2 tablespoons parsley
Chicken stock (optional)

Place the water and the beans in a 3-quart pan, bring to a boil, and cook for exactly 2 minutes. Remove the pan from the heat and let stand covered for 1 hour. In a saucepan, sauté the onions and leeks in the butter and add to the beans along with the bay leaves, sage, thyme, and pepper. Simmer the mixture uncovered for 1½ hours, then purée and set aside.* Toss the eggplant cubes in a bowl with a dash of salt, let stand for 30 minutes, and drain. Sauté the eggplant in the oil and toss with the garlic, tomatoes, and reserved tomato juice. Bring the bean mixture to a boil, add the eggplant, the sliced sausage, and the remaining herbs.

If the soup is too thick, add chicken stock or water to reach desired consistency. When heated through, serve in large bowls.

At this point, the soup may be frozen and stored for later preparation.

Serves 4–6

Liz Kuhlman

Onion Soup Gratinée

An incomparable beginning to a formal dinner or meals en famille —

12 medium red onions, sliced thinly on the
    diagonal
2 tablespoons butter
¼ cup olive oil
1 teaspoon sugar
Salt to taste
3 tablespoons flour
3½ cups chicken broth
4½ cups beef broth
½ cup dry white wine
½ teaspoon Dijon mustard
¼ cup cognac

12 slices French bread, toasted
12 slices Gruyère cheese
Parmesan cheese, grated

Gently sauté the onions in the butter and oil, sprinkle with sugar, and toss to brown. Add the salt and flour and stir until blended thoroughly. Remove the pan from the heat, transfer the mixture to a kettle or stock pot, and add the broths, wine, and mustard. Partially cover the soup and simmer for 30–40 minutes.*

Taste and correct the seasonings, add the cognac, and stir well. In individual ovenproof bowls, place a slice of toasted French bread and a slice of Gruyère. Pour the soup over the cheese, sprinkle the Parmesan over the soup, and bake in a 325° F. oven for 25–30 minutes. Serve immediately.

At this point, the soup may be frozen and stored for later preparation.
Serves 12

Aileen Kleiman

Minestrone Romano

A variation of the Italian classic —

2 tablespoons salt pork or bacon, diced
½ cup ham or prosciutto, diced
1 bunch green onions (with tops), sliced
2 cloves garlic, minced
2 beef bouillon cubes
2½ quarts hot water
1 6-ounce can tomato paste
1 cup carrots, diced
1 cup cabbage, shredded
½ cup celery, diced
½ cup turnips, diced
1 1-pound can red kidney beans

½ cup pasta, uncooked (Acini de Pepe, broken macaroni, or spaghetti is recommended)
½ cup hearty Burgundy
Salt and pepper to taste
Parmesan cheese, freshly grated
½ cup fresh spinach, chopped

In a large, heavy pot, brown the meat over medium heat about 10 minutes. Add the onions and garlic and cook for 2 minutes more. Add the bouillon cubes, water, tomato paste, and vegetables, ex-
cept for the beans and the spinach, and cook for approximately 15 minutes (the vegetables should still be crisp).* Add the kidney beans and pasta, bring to a boil, and cook for 5 minutes. Add the wine and salt and pepper to taste. Serve in large bowls, each sprinkled with Parmesan and a spoonful of fresh spinach.

At this point, the soup may be frozen and stored for later preparation.
Serves 10

Delphine J. Andrews

Avgolemono

Serve this extraordinary egg and lemon soup to create an ambience à la grecque.

2 quarts rich chicken broth
½ cup raw rice
4 eggs, beaten
Juice of 2 lemons (approximately ½ cup)
Salt and pepper to taste

In a saucepan, bring the chicken broth to a boil, add the rice, cook until the rice is tender (about 20 minutes), and remove from the heat. In a bowl, add the lemon juice to the beaten eggs in a slow stream, whisking constantly. Gradually add 1 cup of the hot broth to the eggs, taking care that the heat of the broth does not cook
the eggs. When blended, add the egg mixture to the remaining broth and rice, stirring constantly. Over moderate heat, bring the soup almost to a boil, season to taste, and serve in warmed bowls.
Serves 4–6

Mary Ellen Johnson

Caribbean Black Bean Soup

A superb offering recalling the warmth of island suns —

Water
1 pound black or turtle beans
4 tablespoons bacon drippings
3 large onions, chopped
2 cloves garlic, minced
4 fresh or canned tomatoes, mashed
1 teaspoon oregano
1/2 teaspoon cumin
1/4 teaspoon thyme
1/8 teaspoon marjoram
1 bay leaf
Pinch of coriander
3 ham hocks, halved
1 quart beef broth
1/3 cup dry sherry
Salt and pepper to taste
3–4 tablespoons white wine vinegar
Optional garnishes (see below)

In a 10-quart pot, add water to cover the beans and soak overnight (or cover the beans with boiling water and let soak for 2 hours). After soaking, cover the pot and let the beans simmer for 2 hours or just until tender. Heat the bacon drippings in a large skillet, add the onions, and cook until they begin to take on color. Add the garlic, tomatoes, and seasonings, cook for 3 minutes, and set aside.

Add the onion mixture, ham hocks, and beef broth to the cooked beans. Stir in the sherry and salt and pepper to taste. Partially cover the pot and simmer for 2 hours more, stirring occasionally. Remove the ham hocks, trim the fat, and cut the meat into bite-sized pieces. If the beans are still whole, purée the soup a little at a time in a food processor or blender. Return the soup and meat to the pot, reheat, and stir in the vinegar. The soup may be served with a variety of garnishes such as hard-cooked egg, green onion, lemon, radishes, or capers.

Serves 6–8

W. Hawkins Ferry

Red Snapper Chowder

An Italian classic unequaled in rich flavor —

2 16-ounce cans stewed tomatoes
2 8-ounce cans tomato sauce
2 medium potatoes, peeled and cut into
    1/2-inch cubes
2 onions, chopped coarsely
2 green peppers, seeded and diced
1–2 large cloves garlic, minced
1 bay leaf
1/3 cup fresh parsley, minced
1 teaspoon Italian herb seasoning
1/2 teaspoon salt
Pepper to taste
2 1/2 pounds fillet of red snapper (or any
    firm-fleshed fish), cut into large pieces
1/2 pound small to medium shrimp, cooked
1 6 1/2-ounce can chopped clams, drained

In a 3-quart saucepan, combine the tomatoes, tomato sauce, potatoes, onions, green peppers, garlic, bay leaf, parsley, Italian herb seasoning, salt, and pepper and bring to a boil over medium heat. Reduce the heat, cover, and simmer until the vegetables are barely tender (approximately 30 minutes). Add the red snapper, shrimp, and clams and simmer for 20 minutes or until the snapper flakes easily with a fork. Taste, adjust seasonings, and serve.

Serves 6

Eleanor Mecke

Greek, *Column Krater*, 540/530 B.C., ceramic, black-figure ware, h. 40.7 x diam. 34.2 cm. Founders Society Purchase, Membership Fund (63.17).

Mexican Fish Soup

A trio of tastes combines to create this festive offering.

1 tablespoon olive or corn oil
1 cup onion, chopped
½ teaspoon garlic, chopped
2 cups tomatoes (preferably canned Italian
*   tomatoes with juice), diced*
2 carrots, cut into ½-inch chunks
5 stalks celery, cut into ½-inch chunks
7–8 cups Fish Stock
*   (recipe follows)*
1 teaspoon salt
½ teaspoon ground pepper
4 bay leaves
2 potatoes, cut into ½-inch cubes (optional)
1 fillet of scrod, flounder, monkfish, sea
*   bass, or red snapper, skinned and cut*
*   into 1-inch pieces*
12–18 raw shrimp, peeled, deveined, and
*   halved lengthwise*
6–12 raw oysters
6–12 mussels or clams (or any fresh
*   seafood), scrubbed*
Salsa Cruda
*   (recipe follows)*
2 avocados, peeled and cubed
Lime wedges
Tabasco or other hot sauce (optional)

Note: This is a three-part recipe, most of which may be done in advance and completed 30–40 minutes prior to serving.

Heat the oil in a large pot, add the onion, and cook until transparent. Add the garlic and stir briefly before adding the tomatoes, carrots, celery, and fish stock. Add salt and pepper to taste and the bay leaves, bring to a boil, reduce the heat, and simmer for 15 minutes. Add the potatoes and cook 20 minutes longer or until the potatoes are tender. Add the fish, simmer about 3 minutes, and remove the bay leaves.

When ready to serve, bring the soup to a boil, add the shrimp, oysters, and mussels or clams, and cook for 3–5 minutes or until the shells open (discard any mussels or clams that have not opened). Ladle the soup into bowls and add 1–2 teaspoons of the cold *Salsa Cruda* to each serving. Garnish the soup with avocado and serve with lime wedges to be squeezed into the soup. Tabasco or another hot sauce may also be added to taste.

Serves 8

Fish Stock

3 pounds fish bones (with heads and gills
*   removed)*
2 quarts water
1 cup dry white wine
1 onion, peeled and quartered
*   (approximately ¾ cup)*
¾ cup celery tops, chopped coarsely
1 clove garlic, quartered
1 bay leaf

Combine all of the ingredients in a soup kettle and bring to a boil over medium heat. Cover and simmer for approximately 1½ hours, skimming the surface of the stock several times. Allow the mixture to cool, strain through a fine sieve, and restrain through cheesecloth to obtain a clear broth.

Yields approximately 2 quarts

Salsa Cruda

2 fresh tomatoes (approximately 1 pound),
*   left unpeeled*
¾ cup onion, chopped
Salt to taste
⅓ cup cilantro or parsley, chopped
1–4 tablespoons fresh green chilies (hot or
*   mild), chopped (or canned hot peppers*
*   to taste)*

Halve the tomatoes, squeeze gently to remove the seeds, and cut into small cubes. Combine the tomato cubes with the remaining ingredients and chill in the refrigerator.

Note: The sauce may be made in advance and stored in the refrigerator until needed.

Yields approximately 2½ cups

Doris Burton

Etruscan, *Ladle*, 500 B.C., bronze, 27.3 cm.
Gift of Mrs. Lillian Henkel Haass (51.73).

Bouillabaisse

No aroma could surpass that of this soup from Provençal.

1 large onion, chopped
2 leeks (white portion only), chopped
2 cloves garlic, crushed
½ cup butter
1 cup dry white wine
1 teaspoon saffron
1 bay leaf
1 1-pound can peeled, chopped tomatoes
    (with liquid)
2 cans condensed chicken broth
2 pounds fillet of sole, halibut, flounder, or
    sea bass
1 frozen lobster tail
6 mussels, scrubbed
20 scallops
15 shelled shrimp
Salt and pepper to taste
Aioli (recipe follows)

In a large pot, sauté the onion, leeks, and garlic in the butter until golden. Add the wine, herbs, and tomatoes and simmer briefly. Stir in the broth, bring to a boil, and simmer for 20 minutes. Cut the fish fillets into small pieces and the lobster tail horizontally into slices, add to the soup with the mussels, scallops, and shrimp, and simmer for 10 minutes.* Season with salt and pepper, remove the bay leaf, and serve with *Aioli.*

    Discard any mussels that do not open.

    Serves 6-8 as an entrée (or 10-14 as a first course)

Aioli

2 cloves garlic, crushed
1 shallot, minced
Dash of cayenne pepper
Dash of curry powder
½ teaspoon tarragon
¼ teaspoon thyme
1 pint mayonnaise
2 tablespoons gin

In a small bowl, combine all of the ingredients, blend thoroughly, and place in the refrigerator to chill for at least 2 hours. Serve on the side with *Bouillabaisse* or add a dollop of sauce to each bowl of soup.

    Yields 2 cups

Francine Kaplan

Goodnow and Jenks, American (in partnership 1887/88-1905), *Candlesticks,* 1890/1900, sterling silver, h. 23.5 cm. Founders Society Purchase with funds from Mr. and Mrs. Charles Theron Van Dusen in memory of Charles Theron Van Dusen (1984.7.1-.2).

Portuguese Fish Chowder

A fragrant blend of firm fish and herbs —

¼ cup salt pork, cubed
1 onion, chopped
4 cups cold water
3 cups potatoes, diced
1 teaspoon salt
¼ teaspoon pepper
½ teaspoon saffron
1 tablespoon vinegar
1½ pounds lean fish (haddock, flounder,
    etc.), cut into chunks
2 cups milk or heavy cream

Sauté the pork in a deep, heavy kettle, turning occasionally until only crisp pork bits remain, remove the bits, and reserve. In the remaining hot fat, sauté the onion slowly until golden. Add the water, potatoes, seasonings, and vinegar and boil until the potatoes are half done (about 10 minutes). Add the fish and simmer until tender. Add the milk or cream and cook until the soup is hot but not boiling. Stir in the pork bits and serve.

    Serves 4-6

Thayer Laurie

SALADS

S alads take many forms, from combinations of crisp greens and colorful vegetables to molded gelatin creations, blends of fruits, meats, nuts, seafood — the possibilities are indeed endless! So, too, are the dressings conceived to complement salads. Included here, with dressings that range from subtle and smooth to tart and tangy, are a cornucopia of salads to please every palate.

A lush variety of fruits and vegetables abound in the fresh-tasting salads found in this chapter. Such ripe abundance is mirrored in the early eighteenth-century painting *Summer,* in which Alexandre François Desportes depicted the choicest crops from an entire summer's harvest set in a natural frame of large blossoms. Fruit and flowers form a lovely garland around the silver *Bowl* by American artist Myer Myers. He employed the repoussé technique of hammering a design into relief from the inside of the bowl in order to create a feeling of richness and lavish growth. Karl Schmidt-Rottluff, a twentieth-century German Expressionist artist, made several studies using readily available fresh vegetables. His simply composed yet vibrant works, such as *Tomatoes and Cucumber,* combine contrasting colors and forms to create lively but well-balanced compositions.

Alexandre François Desportes, French, 1661-1743, *Summer* (detail), 1711, oil on canvas, 144.1 x 113 cm. Founders Society Purchase, Elizabeth L. Heavenrich Bequest Fund, Mr. and Mrs. Benson Ford Fund, and Eleanor Clay Ford Fund (65.393).

Anna's Salad

An excellent choice for luncheon parties and light suppers —

1 shallot, chopped
1 tablespoon Dijon mustard
Juice of 2 lemons (approximately 6 tablespoons)
8 tablespoons heavy cream
6 medium heads endive

1 head Bibb lettuce
6 tablespoons bay shrimp
6 king crab legs, cut into 2-inch pieces
8 sections grapefruit

In a jar, combine the chopped shallot, mustard, lemon juice, and cream and shake well. Toss the remaining ingredients in a large salad bowl, add the dressing, toss again, and serve.

Serves 6

Pauline Young

Chicken Salad Jewel Ring

A buffet favorite as attractive as it is appetizing —

2 envelopes unflavored gelatin
1 cup cranberry juice cocktail
1 1-pound can whole cranberry sauce
1 tablespoon lemon juice
¾ cup cold water
1 tablespoon soy sauce
1 cup mayonnaise
1½ cups cooked chicken (white meat), diced
½ cup celery, diced
⅓ cup toasted almonds, chopped

In a saucepan, sprinkle one envelope of the gelatin over the cranberry juice to soften. Cook over low heat, stirring constantly, until the gelatin dissolves. Break up the whole cranberry sauce and stir into the gelatin mixture along with the lemon juice, mixing well. Pour into a 6-cup ring mold and chill until almost firm.

In a separate saucepan, sprinkle the second envelope of gelatin over the cold water to soften and cook over low heat until dissolved. Remove the pan from the heat, stir in the soy sauce, let cool slightly, and gradually whisk in the mayonnaise. Blend in the chicken, celery, and almonds and spoon the mixture on top of the chilled cranberry layer. Return to the refrigerator to chill until firm. Unmold onto a plate covered with salad greens and serve immediately.

Serves 6

Kay Hoff

Cold Curried Rice Salad

An essence of the exotic East pervades this dish.

⅔ cups oil
⅓ cup vinegar
Salt and pepper to taste
¼ teaspoon dry mustard
1 clove garlic (optional)
1 cup raw rice, cooked in salted water
15 radishes, sliced
2–3 carrots, sliced
1 green pepper, diced
1 red onion, diced
2 stalks celery, diced

1 head cauliflower, broken into flowerets
1 small bunch fresh parsley, chopped
1 cup mayonnaise
2–3 tablespoons curry powder
2 6-ounce jars marinated artichoke hearts
Black olives
Capers

Mix together the oil, vinegar, salt, pepper, mustard, and garlic and combine with the cooked rice while it is still warm. Stir in the vegetables and set aside. Blend the mayonnaise with the curry powder and add to the rice mixture. Mound the salad in a large bowl or on a platter and garnish with the artichoke hearts, olives, and capers.

Serves 12–14

Julia Henshaw

Belgian Endive and Orange Salad

The perfect Continental accent to any meal —

2½ tablespoons white wine vinegar
7 tablespoons walnut oil
1 tablespoon light cream
Salt and pepper to taste
1 red onion, diced
4 heads Belgian endive
2 bunches watercress
2 oranges, cut into segments

Combine the vinegar and oil, whisk in the cream, and add salt and pepper to taste. Gather the diced onion in a towel, wring out as much juice as possible, run under cold water, and wring again. Add the onions to the dressing and set aside to marinate for a few hours before completing the salad. Cut the top two inches from the endive leaves and arrange to form two-thirds of a circle on each salad plate. Cut the top two inches from the watercress and arrange to complete the circles. Chop the remaining endive into ¼-inch pieces and place in a bowl. Add the orange segments and chilled dressing, toss well, and mound in the center of each plate.

Serves 4

Lainie and Max Pincus

Crab Salad Contessa

Cool and delicious, especially in summer's heat —

¼ cup plus 1 tablespoon fresh lemon juice
½ cup capers, drained
Freshly ground pepper
4 cups crabmeat chunks (cooked, frozen, or canned)
1 medium jícama, peeled, sliced, and cut into julienne strips (or 1 8-ounce can sliced water chestnuts, drained)
12 radishes
1 cup mayonnaise
1 cup plain yogurt
2 heads Bibb lettuce, chilled

1 4-ounce package alfalfa sprouts, chilled
24 pitted olives, chilled

Combine ¼ cup of the lemon juice, the capers, and the pepper, add the crabmeat and jícama, and marinate overnight. Wash, trim, and cut the radishes into fans or roses. Chill the radishes in water to open and reserve in the refrigerator. Mix together the mayonnaise, yogurt, and remaining tablespoon of lemon juice and refrigerate until needed.

Assemble the salad just before serving by stirring the dressing gently into the crabmeat mixture. Arrange the lettuce on chilled plates, make nests of the alfalfa sprouts, and mound the crabmeat salad in each nest. Garnish with chilled olives and radishes.

Serves 12

Phyllis McLean

Chicken Salad Mandarin

The tang of oranges adds zest to this salad.

3 cups cooked chicken or turkey, diced
1½ cups long-grain rice, cooked and chilled
1 11-ounce can mandarin oranges, drained
1 cup celery, diced
½ cup mayonnaise
½ cup creamy French salad dressing
½ teaspoon curry powder

½ teaspoon salt
¼ teaspoon pepper

In a large bowl, combine the chicken, rice, oranges, and celery. In a smaller bowl, combine the mayonnaise, French dressing, and spices and blend well. Pour the salad dressing over the chicken mixture and toss lightly. Chill for at least 1 hour before serving.

Serves 6–8

Lucie Kelly

Turnip Salad Lillian

Crisp vegetables tossed in a tart dressing —

¼ teaspoon prepared mustard
¼ teaspoon prepared horseradish
1 tablespoon sour cream
½ cup mayonnaise
1 tablespoon dill or parsley (fresh or dried),
    minced
Salt and white pepper to taste
6 raw turnips, peeled and cut into julienne
    strips

Bibb lettuce
2–3 tablespoons capers
2 tablespoons pine nuts
Pimento

Combine the mustard, horseradish, sour cream, mayonnaise, dill or parsley, and salt and pepper, blend well, and mix with the turnips. Serve the salad mounded on beds of Bibb lettuce sprinkled with the capers and pine nuts and garnished with the pimento.

Serves 4–6

Lillian Shaye-Hirsch

Marinated Mushroom Spring Salad

A piquant way to welcome the fresh days of spring —

1 pound fresh mushrooms, sliced
1 cup celery, sliced thinly
½ cup green pepper, chopped
½ cup green onion, chopped
1 cup olive or salad oil
¼ cup red wine vinegar
2 teaspoons basil

1 teaspoon salt
½ teaspoon garlic, minced
½ teaspoon black pepper, ground coarsely
½ teaspoon sugar

Combine the mushrooms, celery, green pepper, and onions in a large bowl and set aside. Mix together the remaining ingredients, pour over the vegetables, toss well, and chill 6 hours or overnight. Drain the vegetables and serve on beds of lettuce.

Serves 6–8

Mrs. George Pierrot

Green Salad with Chèvre, Apple, and Walnuts

A tangy, fresh companion to soups and entrées —

4–6 rounds chèvre (goat) cheese
    (approximately 2 inches in diameter
    by ½-inch thick)
½ cup olive oil
Thyme or rosemary to taste (fresh or dried)
1 cup fine bread crumbs
4 tablespoons walnut or peanut oil
1 tablespoon white wine vinegar
1 teaspoon Dijon mustard
Salt and pepper to taste
1 head Boston or Bibb lettuce
1–2 heads Belgian endive
1 bunch watercress
½ cup walnut pieces

1 Granny Smith apple, cored and chopped
    but not peeled

Marinate the chèvre in the olive oil and thyme or rosemary for a few hours or overnight. Remove the cheese from the oil, dip in the bread crumbs, and place in a lightly oiled baking dish. Bake in a 400° F. oven for approximately 6 minutes (or until the cheese bubbles gently and is lightly browned).

Combine the oil, vinegar, mustard, salt, and pepper, beat well with a whisk or a fork, and set aside. Toss the lettuce, endive, and watercress with the walnuts, apple, and enough of the vinaigrette to coat lightly. Arrange the mixture on individual salad plates, place a warm cheese round in the center of each plate, and serve with the remaining vinaigrette and a loaf of warm French bread on the side.

Serves 4–6

Anne Spivak

Shrimp and Artichoke Salad

A cool boon to warm-weather entertaining —

1 cup mayonnaise
6 tablespoons capers
2 tablespoons caper juice
1 tablespoon lemon juice
4 cups shrimp, peeled and cooked
3 cups artichoke hearts, quartered
Salt and pepper to taste

In a small bowl, combine the mayonnaise with the capers, caper juice, and lemon juice. Pour the dressing over the shrimp and toss well. Add the artichokes, season with salt and pepper to taste, and mix gently. Chill for 3 hours before serving.

    Serves 6–8

Suzy Farbman

Myer Myers, American, 1723-1795, *Bowl*, ca.1750/60, silver, h. 11.1 x diam. 16.5 cm. Founders Society Purchase, Gibbs-Williams Fund (69.260).

Curried Spinach Salad

Indian spices distinguish this dish.

2 pounds spinach
3 Red or Golden Delicious apples, cored and
   diced
2/3 cup dry-roasted Spanish peanuts
1/2 cup raisins
1/3 cup green onion, sliced thinly
2 tablespoons sesame seeds, toasted lightly
1/2 cup white wine vinegar
2/3 cup salad oil
1 tablespoon chutney, minced

1 teaspoon curry powder
1 teaspoon dry mustard
1 teaspoon salt
1 teaspoon Tabasco sauce

Trim and discard the rough spinach stems. Rinse, pat dry, and break the spinach into bite-sized pieces, wrap in paper toweling, and chill until needed. Combine the apples with the peanuts, raisins, onion, sesame seeds, and spinach. Whisk together the vinegar, salad oil, chutney, curry powder, mustard, salt, and Tabasco sauce, pour over the salad, and toss lightly just before serving.

    Serves 6–8

Anna Van Hull

Green Beans Pierre

This crisp and flavorful dish is a vegetable lover's dream.

1 pound fresh green beans
7–8 small new potatoes
1/2 cup olive oil
2 tablespoons wine vinegar
1/4 teaspoon salt
1/4 teaspoon dry mustard
1/4 teaspoon tarragon
1/4 teaspoon basil
1/2 teaspoon parsley
1/4 teaspoon garlic salt
1/4 teaspoon pepper
2 tablespoons onion, chopped

1–2 fresh tomatoes, chopped coarsely
Lettuce
Caper-stuffed anchovies
Small, ripe olives

Cook the green beans just until tender, drain, and chill in cold water. Peel and cook the new potatoes (be careful not to overcook), drain, and dice. Mix the oil, vinegar, herbs, and seasonings, pour over the beans and potatoes, and chill for at least 1 hour. At serving time, toss the beans and potatoes with the chopped onion and tomatoes and place in a lettuce-lined bowl. Garnish with caper-stuffed anchovies and ripe olives.

    Serves 4

Peggy Winkelman

Wild Duck Salad

Whether made with wild duck or domestic, it's a superlative delight.

2 4½-pound ducks
½–1 teaspoon salt
¼–½ teaspoon freshly ground pepper
1 small clove garlic, crushed
½ teaspoon Dijon mustard
¼ cup port
6 tablespoons red wine vinegar
3 tablespoons fresh orange juice
¼ cup olive oil
½ cup scallions, sliced
2 bunches watercress
2 oranges, sliced thinly
Pickled Beets
    (see recipe p. 118)

Preheat the oven to 350° F. Remove the necks, gizzards, and excess fat from the cavities of the ducks and discard. Cut off the wing tips, prick the skin, and sprinkle inside and out with salt and pepper to taste. Place the ducks on a rack in a roasting pan, bake for 40 minutes, reduce the heat to 275°F., and roast for another 2¾ hours or until the ducks are tender.

Prepare a marinade by combining the garlic, mustard, port, red wine vinegar, orange juice, ½ teaspoon salt, and ¼ teaspoon pepper in a large bowl. Stir to blend, slowly whisk in the olive oil, and set aside.

Remove the ducks from the oven and let stand. When cool enough to handle, gently separate the skin from the ducks by hand or with a sharp knife, trying not to tear the skin. Cut the skin into ½-inch cubes, place on a cookie sheet, and roast in a 275°F. oven until crisp (15–20 minutes). While the skin cracklings are roasting, remove the duck meat from the bones, trim away the fat, and cut into ½-inch cubes. While still warm, place the meat in the marinade and let stand until room temperature (about 15 minutes). Remove the cracklings from the oven, drain on paper towels, and sprinkle with salt and pepper. Mix the cubed duck and marinade with the scallions, mound on beds of watercress, and sprinkle with the skin cracklings. Garnish with orange slices and pickled beets.

Serves 4–6

Betty Muer

Shrimp Macadamia with Orzo

A highlight of our 1984 fundraiser "Under the Stars V" —

20 large shrimp, cooked, shelled, and
    deveined (leave tails intact)
Boiling water
28 snow pea pods
1½ pounds medium shrimp, cooked and
    shelled
15 large white mushrooms, cleaned and
    sliced thinly
1 cup macadamia nuts, chopped
3 tablespoons sweet red onions, diced
½ cup orzo, cooked and drained
Vinaigrette Dressing
    (see recipe p. 22)
3 tablespoons Dijon mustard
Juice of 1 large lemon
2 tablespoons fresh dill
½ cup olive oil

½ cup salad oil
2 egg yolks, beaten lightly
Salt and freshly ground pepper to taste
Arugula or radicchio leaves

Butterfly the large shrimp, make a slit through each near the tail, and insert the tail through the slit so that each shrimp will stand on its own. Refrigerate the shrimp until needed. Blanch the pea pods for 30 seconds in boiling water, plunge into cold water, and drain. Slice each pod diagonally into 3 pieces and combine in a large bowl with the medium shrimp, mushrooms, macadamia nuts, onions, and orzo.

In a jar, combine the vinaigrette dressing, mustard, lemon juice, dill, olive and salad oils, egg yolks, and salt and pepper to taste and shake well. Pour the dressing over the salad and toss lightly. Arrange the arugula or radicchio leaves on salad plates, mound the salad in the center, and garnish with 2 large shrimp each.

Serves 10

The Cookbook Committee

Karl Schmidt-Rottluff, German, 1884–1976, *Tomatoes and Cucumber,* 20th cent., watercolor, 49.8 x 69.8 cm. Founders Society Purchase, Friends of Modern Art Fund (36.43).

Bishie's Rice Salad

A rich and flavorful combination —

1 cup peas (fresh or frozen)
½ teaspoon rosemary
½ teaspoon sugar
1–1½ cups raw white rice, cooked and
*   chilled*
¾ cup celery, sliced thinly
¾ cup slivered almonds, toasted
½ cup raisins
½ cup sour cream
½ cup mayonnaise
4–5 tablespoons chutney, chopped
1 teaspoon curry powder (or to taste)
Salt and pepper to taste

Cook the peas with the rosemary and sugar, drain, and let cool. Transfer the peas to a large bowl and add the rice, celery, almonds, and raisins. In a small bowl, mix together the sour cream, mayonnaise, chutney, curry powder, and salt and pepper, add to the rice mixture, and toss. Taste and adjust the seasonings. Chill at least 8 hours before serving.
    Serves 8

Bishie Beatty

Native American (Eastern Sioux), *Feast Bowl*, ca. 1850, maple and brass tacks, 18.4 x 43.8 x 39.4 cm. Gift of Flint Ink Corporation (81.497).

Ruth's Marinated Salad

Tart flavors combine to complement this blend of vegetables.

1 medium zucchini, washed and dried but
*   not peeled*
½ teaspoon salt
1 medium leek, washed and drained
1 16-ounce can sliced beets, drained
1 16-ounce can artichoke hearts
¾ cup safflower oil combined with
*   2 tablespoons olive oil*
¼ cup red wine vinegar
4 teaspoons Dijon mustard
2 teaspoons dried dill weed
Salt and pepper to taste
Romaine lettuce

Cut the zucchini into julienne strips, sprinkle with ½ teaspoon salt, place in a colander, and set aside for 30 minutes. Cut the leek into julienne strips, add to the zucchini, and set aside in a large bowl. Cut the beets into julienne strips, place in a separate bowl, and set aside. Drain and rinse the artichoke hearts and place in a third bowl. In a small jar, combine the oil, red wine vinegar, mustard, dill weed, and salt and pepper to taste and shake well. Pour some of the vinaigrette dressing over each bowl of vege-tables and marinate for at least 2 hours. Line a salad bowl with the romaine lettuce, mound the beets in the center of the bowl, and cover completely with the zucchini and leek mixture. Garnish with the artichoke hearts.

    Note: This salad may be assembled in advance and kept refrigerated until needed.
    Serves 4–6

Ruth Lefkowitz

Dutch Boy Lettuce

From the Netherlands comes a hot and hearty salad —

4 slices bacon
1 egg, beaten lightly
⅓ cup sour cream
¼ cup vinegar
2 tablespoons sugar
⅛ teaspoon salt
½ head lettuce, torn into pieces

5 ounces fresh spinach, torn into pieces
3 green onions, sliced

In a large skillet, cook the bacon until crisp, drain (reserve 1 tablespoon of the drippings in the skillet), crumble, and set aside. Combine the beaten egg, sour cream, vinegar, sugar, and salt in the skillet with the drippings, heat, and stir until thickened. Add the lettuce, spinach, and onions and toss until well coated. Place the mixture in a salad bowl, sprinkle the crumbled bacon over the top, and serve immediately.
Serves 4–6

Diane Raines

Fabulous Spinach Salad

A superb addition to the variations on a classic —

2 pounds fresh spinach
1 pound fresh bean sprouts
1 8-ounce can water chestnuts, sliced
1 large clove garlic, crushed
½ teaspoon salt
1 teaspoon lemon rind, grated
½ teaspoon paprika
½ teaspoon freshly ground pepper
4 tablespoons tarragon vinegar
¾ cup olive oil

4 tablespoons sour cream
10 slices bacon, cooked to a crisp and crumbled

Wash and dry the spinach and bean sprouts. Remove the large stems and veins from the spinach, tear into bite-sized pieces, combine with the bean sprouts and water chestnuts, and place in the refrigerator to chill. With a whisk or a fork combine the garlic, salt, lemon rind, paprika, pepper, and tarragon vinegar. Gradually mix in the olive oil and sour cream. Pour the dressing over the chilled spinach, sprouts, and water chestnuts, toss well, and sprinkle the crumbled bacon over the top. Serve immediately.
Serves 12

Lee Henkin

Green Salad Mandarin

A wonderful accompaniment to chicken or seafood —

½ cup oil
2 tablespoons tarragon vinegar
¼ teaspoon Tabasco sauce
2 tablespoons sugar
1 teaspoon salt
Freshly ground pepper to taste
1 head lettuce
1 cup celery, chopped

4 green onions, chopped
½ cup slivered almonds, toasted
1 tablespoon parsley, minced
1 11-ounce can mandarin oranges, drained
1 avocado, diced

Combine the oil, tarragon vinegar, Tabasco sauce, sugar, salt, and pepper, blend well, and chill. Break the lettuce into small pieces, add the remaining ingredients and the chilled dressing, and toss to blend before serving.
Serves 6–8

Sue Clippert

Moroccan Eggplant Salad

A tasty treasure from the Near East —

2 medium-sized eggplants (approximately
    1 pound each), peeled
Salt
¼ cup olive oil
3 large tomatoes, peeled, seeded, and
    chopped
2 sweet green peppers, sliced into rings
2–3 cloves garlic, minced
1 tablespoon fresh cilantro or parsley,
    chopped
1 teaspoon sweet paprika
½ teaspoon ground cumin
Juice of ½ lemon

Cut the eggplant into ½-inch slices, sprinkle with salt, and drain in a colander for about 15 minutes. Rinse the eggplant, squeezing gently, and pat dry. In a large skillet, heat the olive oil over high heat, add the eggplant, and sauté until golden brown on both sides (add more oil if needed). Remove the eggplant, allow to cool, and cut into quarters.

Reduce the heat to medium-low, add the tomatoes and green peppers to the skillet, cover, and cook for 10–15 minutes, stirring occasionally. Mash the tomatoes and green peppers with a wooden spoon, add the eggplant, cover again, and cook for 20–25 minutes or until the eggplant is tender. Add the garlic, cilantro, paprika, and cumin and cook uncovered over medium heat, stirring frequently until all liquid has evaporated (approximately 10 minutes). Pour off any excess oil, season with lemon juice, and salt to taste. Serve warm or at room temperature.

Serves 6

Hope Palmer

Lalap

A zesty cucumber salad with the accent of chili peppers —

1 long cucumber, peeled and sliced thinly
1 cup bean sprouts
1 leek, washed and sliced thinly
¼ cup mild vinegar
Salt to taste
Sugar to taste
Dash of red chili peppers, crushed
2 dashes of salad oil
1 teaspoon onion, minced

Combine the cucumber, bean sprouts, and leek in a bowl. In a separate bowl or jar, blend together the vinegar, salt, sugar, chili peppers, salad oil, and onion. Pour the dressing over the vegetables, toss to coat, and serve.

Serves 2–4

Dirk Bakker

Cabbage Salad

A distinguished version of a delicatessen classic —

1 small to medium cabbage, chopped
    coarsely
3 carrots, grated coarsely
2 cucumbers, sliced thinly
1 green pepper, sliced thinly
3 small red onions, sliced thinly
6 tablespoons wine vinegar
6 tablespoons sugar (or to taste)
6 tablespoons salad oil
2 teaspoons salt

Combine all of the vegetables in a deep bowl. Mix together the wine vinegar, sugar, salad oil, and salt and pour over the vegetables. Refrigerate for 24 hours, stirring occasionally.

Serves 8

Sandra Moers

Gorham Manufacturing Company, American, *Two-handled Cup*, 1893, sterling silver, parcel-gilt, 31.9 x 37 x 23.6 cm. Gift of the Honorable Thomas W. Palmer (13.27).

Sardine Salad in Lemon Shells

Delightful served with a light summer soup —

6 large lemons
2 3¾-ounce cans brisling sardines
1 egg, hard-boiled and minced
2–3 tablespoons mayonnaise
1 1-inch ribbon anchovy paste (or 1–2
    anchovies, minced)
Dash of vodka (optional)
Freshly ground pepper to taste
2 tablespoons chives
2 tablespoons parsley, minced

Cut one-third from the top of each lemon. Squeeze the juice from both the top and bottom (taking care not to split the skins), strain, and reserve. With a curled grapefruit knife or spoon, cut the pulp from the lemon shells and discard. Cut thin slices from the bottoms of the shells so they will stand firmly and set the shells aside.

Drain most of the oil from the sardines, place the sardines in a bowl with the egg, and mash thoroughly to blend.

Stir the mayonnaise and anchovy paste together with the vodka and blend into the sardine mixture. Season to taste with the reserved lemon juice,* pepper, and chives. Spoon the salad into the lemon shells and garnish with the chopped parsley.

A generous portion of the lemon juice may be added, but not all will be needed.

Serves 6

Jean W. Hudson

Lentil Salad

An excellent traveler, excellent for picnics —

5 cups water
1 pound lentils
2 teaspoons salt
¾ cup salad or olive oil
1 large onion, chopped
2 stalks celery, chopped
½ cup green pepper, chopped
2 tablespoons red wine vinegar
⅔ teaspoon salt

1 bunch parsley, chopped
1 egg, hard-boiled and chopped

Bring the water to a boil, add the lentils and salt, reduce the heat, and cover. Simmer for 25 minutes or until the lentils are just tender, drain, toss with 4 tablespoons of the oil, and let stand to cool. Combine the lentils with the onion, celery, and green pepper and set aside. Mix together the remaining oil, red wine vinegar, and salt, pour over the salad, toss to blend, and refrigerate overnight. Garnish with the parsley and egg.

Serves 12–16

Vivian Richards

Spaghettini Salad

This salad is a sheer delight on even the hottest day.

1 pound spaghettini, broken into shorter
    lengths
Water, salted
½ cucumber, chopped
1 bunch green onions, chopped
½ large green pepper, chopped
1 bunch radishes, sliced
1 2-ounce jar pimentos, chopped
4 eggs, hard-boiled and chopped
1 large pinch oregano
1½ teaspoons salt

¾ teaspoon pepper
1 teaspoon sugar
½ teaspoon celery seed
2 cups mayonnaise
⅓ pint sour cream
4 tablespoons Durkee's Dressing
1 tablespoon prepared mustard
⅓ pint half-and-half

Cook the spaghettini in boiling, salted water, rinse in cold water, drain, and set aside. Combine the vegetables and the eggs in a large bowl, add the pasta, oregano, salt, pepper, sugar, and celery seed, and toss. Mix the mayonnaise, sour cream, dressing, mustard, and half-and-half, pour over the salad, and toss until thoroughly blended. Chill the salad in the refrigerator before serving.

Serves 12

Jan Dailey

PASTA, RICE, CHEESE, AND EGG DISHES

*G*rains have played an important role in every culture throughout history, as evidenced by ancient Egyptian reliefs recording offerings of grain and such modern works as this *Woman with Grain.* The latter is part of the upper register of the East Wall of a group of frescoes called *Detroit Industry,* which were designed for the Detroit Institute of Arts and painted in the museum's Garden Court by Diego Rivera in 1932 and 1933. The grain held by this female symbol of fertility, and fruits and vegetables painted in the lower register side panels of the wall, were chosen by the artist because they are indigenous to Michigan.

Grains are used in many foods. Pasta, made from wheat paste, and rice, long a staple of Asian diets, may have been introduced to America by Thomas Jefferson. Delicious on their own or in innumerable combinations, these versatile foods have become an important part of the American diet along with such products as cheese and eggs.

From ancient times and in many cultures, the egg has symbolized infinity and its function and form have been considered perfect. Certainly many artists have been intrigued by the egg's shape for it is not infrequently found in art as evidenced in *Still Life, San Francisco, California* by twentieth-century photographer Ansel Adams. The *Still Life* by Jean-Siméon Chardin is another excellent example: the curve of the eggs is reiterated by the rounded base of the kettle, its handle, the turned wooden box, and the bowl with handle. The use of these simple shapes creates an atmosphere of quiet dignity and domestic charm.

Jean-Siméon Chardin, French, 1699-1779, *Still Life* (detail), ca. 1732, oil on canvas, 16.8 x 21 cm. Bequest of Robert H. Tannahill (70.164).

Pàglia e Fièno a la Barese

Though the origin of the title, which may be translated as "Straw and Hay," is now lost, this delightful toss of pasta and vegetables traditionally was served at betrothal banquets and thus is prepared often for special occasions.

5 ounces egg pasta
5 ounces spinach pasta
20 fresh mussels, scrubbed
½ cup butter
2 cloves garlic, minced
3 ounces turnips, peeled and cut into
   julienne strips
2 fresh basil leaves
4 ounces mushrooms, sliced finely
8 cherry tomatoes, halved
¼ cup dry white wine
¼ cup Parmesan cheese (optional)

Cook the egg and spinach pasta separately, drain, rinse in cold water, and set aside. Steam the mussels for 5 minutes, discard any that have not opened, remove the meat from those remaining, and set aside. Melt the butter in a frying pan and sauté the garlic until golden. Add the turnips and basil, stir gently, and cook for 1 minute only. Add the drained pasta to the pan and cook for 2 minutes, stirring frequently. Add the mussels, mushrooms, and tomatoes, stir in the wine, and continue to cook just until the pasta is thoroughly heated. Garnish with Parmesan cheese and serve immediately.

Serves 4

Joseph Beato

Cold Pasta New Orleans Style

A tasty and colorful summer dish —

¼ cup wine vinegar
2 teaspoons Dijon mustard
2 teaspoons garlic, minced
1 teaspoon paprika
Salt and pepper to taste
1 cup olive oil
½ pound vermicelli or spaghettini
Water
2 cups cooked chicken, diced
1 cup fresh mayonnaise
Mushrooms à la Grecque
   (recipe follows)
12 small whole beets, cooked and drained
1 9-ounce package frozen artichoke hearts,
   cooked and drained
1 avocado, peeled, seeded, and cut into
   wedges
12 cherry tomatoes or 2 medium tomatoes,
   cut into wedges
3 scallions, chopped
2 sprigs fresh parsley, chopped

In a large bowl, combine the wine vinegar, mustard, garlic, paprika, and salt and pepper to taste. Using a whisk, gradually incorporate the oil into the vinegar mixture and set aside. Cook the pasta in boiling salted water, drain, and transfer to a bowl. Shake the dressing and toss one-third of the dressing with the pasta. Let the pasta cool, cover, and refrigerate several hours or overnight.

Add the chicken and mayonnaise to the pasta, toss again, and mound on a platter or on individual plates. Coat the *Mushrooms à la Grecque*, beets, artichoke hearts, and avocado wedges with the remaining dressing and arrange over the pasta. Add the tomatoes and sprinkle the salad with the chopped scallions and parsley.

Serves 6–8

Mushrooms à la Grecque

½ pound small mushrooms
1½ tablespoons lemon juice
4½ tablespoons olive oil
½ teaspoon coriander seeds
1 small clove garlic, crushed
Salt and pepper to taste
2 tablespoons chicken broth

In a small pan, combine all of the ingredients, cover, and cook over low heat for 7 minutes. Uncover and cook the mushrooms over high heat for 5 minutes more. Set the mushrooms aside and let cool.

Yields 1½–2 cups

Judith Weston

Giovanni Francesco Susini, Italian, active 1592–1646, *Bacchus and a Young Satyr*, ca. 1640, bronze, 50 x 22.9 x 20.3 cm. Founders Society Purchase, New Endowment Fund (82.27).

Pasta Carciòfi

A feast of angel hair and artichoke hearts —

Juice of 3 lemons
Zest of 1½ lemons, cut into julienne strips
2 1-pound cans artichoke hearts, quartered
    (or the equivalent of frozen artichoke
    hearts)
1 cup plus 1 tablespoon olive oil
2 cups chicken broth
2 tablespoons garlic, minced
2 cups parsley, chopped
Salt and pepper
6 ounces angel hair pasta
1 tablespoon salt

Combine the lemon juice and zest, artichoke hearts, 1 cup of the olive oil, chicken broth, garlic, and parsley and boil for 7 minutes. Season to taste with salt and pepper and set aside. In a large kettle, cook the pasta 1 minute in boiling salted water to which 1 tablespoon of olive oil has been added. Rinse the pasta in cold water, drain, and toss with the artichoke sauce. Serve hot or refrigerate and serve chilled.

Serves 6

John I. Bloom

Shrimp Pasta Primavera

A superb combination of the yield of the garden and the fruits of the sea —

¾ cup asparagus, peeled and sliced
    diagonally into ½-inch pieces
¾ cup small carrots, pared and sliced
    diagonally into ½-inch pieces
5 ounces frozen peas (or ¾ cup fresh peas)
½ pound egg noodles
Water, salted
1 tablespoon oil
2 egg yolks
1½ cups light cream
3 tablespoons unsalted butter
1 clove garlic, minced
½ cup Parmesan cheese, grated
1 pound shelled shrimp, cleaned and cooked
Chives or parsley, chopped
Freshly ground pepper

Cook the asparagus, carrots, and peas separately, rinse in cold water, drain, and combine in a large bowl. Cook the noodles in boiling, salted water to which 1 tablespoon oil has been added, drain, and set aside. Beat the egg yolks with a little of the cream and set aside.

In a large pot, melt the butter, add the garlic, and sauté for about 30 seconds. Add the remaining cream and the cheese, bring to a boil, and cook for 30 seconds. Slowly stir in the egg yolk and cream mixture, blending thoroughly. Add the egg noodles, vegetables, and shrimp and toss to coat. Garnish with the chives or parsley and serve with additional Parmesan and freshly ground pepper.

Note: If desired, a greater variety of vegetables may be used or ham or prosciutto may be substituted for the shrimp.

Serves 4–5

Marjorie Peebles-Meyers

Penne all'Arrabbiata

Due to its elongated shape, the pasta used in this dish is called penne, meaning "pens" or "pencils." Arrabbiata means "enraged" or "angry" and refers to the hot, spicy flavor of Penne all'Arrabbiata. These "enraged pens" will write their way onto any menu!

¼ cup olive oil
½ teaspoon garlic, chopped
1½ pounds sweet Italian sausage, casing removed
1 cup parsley, chopped
1 teaspoon basil (or 2–3 leaves fresh)
1 teaspoon oregano
1 teaspoon thyme
1 tablespoon fennel seeds
1 teaspoon red pepper, crushed
½ cup dry red wine
2 28-ounce cans Italian-style tomatoes, drained and chopped
Salt and pepper
1 15-ounce can artichoke hearts, drained and halved
1 pound Italian penne
4 quarts water, salted
2 tablespoons butter
1 cup pecorino cheese, grated
1 cup Parmesan cheese, grated

Preheat the oven to 350°F. Heat the oil in a skillet and sauté the garlic until golden. Add the sausage in small chunks, brown over medium heat, and drain off the fat. Add the herbs and red pepper, cook for 5 minutes, stirring constantly, then add the wine and cook over high heat until the wine has evaporated. Stir in the tomatoes, salt, and pepper, cook for 30 minutes, and set aside.*

Place the artichoke hearts in a dish, sprinkle with salt, and let sit at room temperature for 30 minutes. Cook the penne in 4 quarts of boiling salted water for 10 minutes and drain. Melt the butter in a casserole dish and add a small amount of the sauce. Add the penne, sprinkle with one-half of the combined cheeses, and blend while slowly adding more sauce and one-half of the artichokes. Top with the remaining sauce, artichokes, and cheese and bake for 15–20 minutes or until heated through.

*The sauce may be prepared in advance and kept frozen until needed.

Serves 8

Andrew Camden

Pasta al Quattro Formàggi

A tempting dish, "Pasta with Four Cheeses" tests the palate with its range of subtleties.

¾ pound vermicelli or spaghettini
½ cup butter
1 cup milk
1 teaspoon cornstarch
¼ pound each Edam, provolone, Gruyère, and fontina cheeses, diced
Parmesan cheese, grated

Cook the pasta al dente, drain, toss with 2 tablespoons of the butter, and set aside. Melt the remaining butter in a saucepan. Combine the milk and the cornstarch, stir into the melted butter, and cook, stirring constantly, for 5 minutes or until smooth and thick. Add the cheeses, except for the Parmesan, and cook for 3 minutes or until almost completely melted. Toss the cheese sauce with the pasta, top with the grated Parmesan, and serve.

Serves 6

Mrs. J. Denton Anderson

Persian or Mesopotamian, *Ewer*, late 7th-early 8th cent., bronze, h. 47 x diam. 16 cm. Founders Society Purchase, Hill Memorial Fund (76.96).

Spaghetti alla Carbonara

This dish originated with the charcoal workers (carbonai) in the mountains of northern Italy. Our recipe was obtained from an Italian professor in Rome and deserves a starring role in any meal.

8 thick slices bacon, cut into ½-inch strips
3 tablespoons olive oil
2–4 cloves garlic, minced
½ teaspoon red pepper flakes (optional)
½ cup heavy cream
3 eggs
½ cup fresh Parmesan cheese, grated
2 tablespoons fresh Romano or pecorino cheese, grated
½ teaspoon salt
Pepper, ground coarsely

1 pound pasta, cooked al dente
½ teaspoon paprika (optional)
2 tablespoons parsley, chopped (optional)

Lightly brown the bacon in the oil, pour off one-half of the grease, add the garlic and pepper flakes, and sauté for 1 minute. Stir the cream gently into the bacon mixture, keeping the mixture at a low simmer. In a bowl, beat together the eggs, cheeses, and salt and pepper. Pour the cream and bacon mixture over the hot pasta and toss. Add the beaten egg mixture and toss again thoroughly. Top with the paprika and the parsley and serve immediately.
Serves 4

Peg Tallet

Middle Eastern Rice and Vermicelli

A subtle blend of textures and tastes —

¼ cup butter
⅔ cup vermicelli or spaghettini
1 cup raw rice
2 cups chicken stock
Pepper to taste
3 green onions, chopped
Pine nuts, toasted

Melt the butter in a large frying pan. Break the vermicelli into 1-inch pieces, add to the pan, and stir until well browned. Stir in the rice and brown lightly. Add the chicken stock and pepper, bring to a boil, cover, and cook for 20 minutes over low heat, stirring once or twice or until all of the liquid is absorbed. Serve the rice and vermicelli topped with the chopped green onions and toasted pine nuts.

Note: Beef or lamb broth may be substituted for the chicken stock, or, for a slightly different flavor, bits of meat may be added to the rice mixture just before serving.
Serves 6

Marianne Schwartz

Rice with Green Chilies

Almost as full of surprises as a holiday piñata —

1 cup raw rice, cooked
2 cups sour cream
Salt and pepper to taste
½ pound Monterey Jack cheese, cubed
2 4-ounce cans green chilies, chopped

2 tablespoons butter
½ cup Parmesan cheese, grated

Combine the cooked rice with the sour cream and season to taste. Arrange one-half of the rice in a shallow, 1½-quart casserole dish. Sprinkle the rice with the Monterey Jack and green chilies, cover with the remaining rice, dot with the butter, and sprinkle with the Parmesan. Bake in a 350°F. oven for 30 minutes or until the top has browned.
Serves 6–8

Elizabeth Rentenbach

South Pacific Rice

A very colorful accompaniment to pork or chicken —

3 tablespoons butter
1½ cups raw rice
¼ teaspoon ginger
¼ teaspoon nutmeg
2 green onions, chopped
4 slices bacon, cooked and crumbled
4 tablespoons green pepper, chopped
2 stalks celery, chopped

1 large tomato, skinned, seeded, and
    chopped
½ cup raisins
¼ cup slivered almonds
3 cups chicken broth

In a 3-quart, heavy, ovenproof dish, melt the butter, combine all of the remaining ingredients, and bring to a boil over medium heat. Cover the dish and place in a 350°F. oven for 20 minutes, remove, stir gently, and return to bake for 10 minutes more or until done.
    Serves 8–10

Ruth Holcomb

Rice and Nuts

A fine, nutty flavor makes this dish distinctive.

¾ cup whole almonds
¼ cup pine nuts
2 tablespoons oil
1½ cups rice
2¼ cups water
1 teaspoon salt

4 tablespoons honey
2 tablespoons soy or tamari sauce

Brown the almonds and the pine nuts in the oil and set aside. Place the rice, water, and salt in a heavy pan, bring to a boil, cover, and reduce the heat. Cook the rice until the water is completely absorbed (approximately 15 minutes). Let the rice sit, covered, away from the heat until ready to use. In a skillet, combine the nuts and the rice, add the honey and soy or tamari sauce, reheat, and serve.
    Serves 6–8

Barbara Carson-McHale

East Bay Rice

A nourishing combination flavored with herbs and topped with pine nuts —

2 tablespoons butter
1 onion, chopped
1 cup raw white rice
2 teaspoons Fines Herbes
2 cups chicken broth
1–2 tablespoons vegetable oil
2 eggs
½ cup green beans, cooked and diced
    (or peas, cooked)
2–3 tomatoes, diced
⅓ cup pine nuts
⅓ cup parsley, chopped

In a heavy pot with a tight-fitting lid, melt the butter and sauté the onion and rice until the rice becomes opaque. Add the Fines Herbes and the broth, bring to a boil, cover, and reduce the heat. Simmer for 12 minutes and check to see if the liquid has been absorbed (if it has not been completely absorbed, return the cover to the pan and remove from the heat for 2–3 minutes).

While the rice is cooking, heat the vegetable oil in a skillet and make two thin omelettes as follows: beat one egg at a time, pour into the skillet, swirl to coat the interior of the pan, and cook until set. Roll each omelette, slice into thin strips, and add to the rice along with the vegetables and pine nuts. Garnish with chopped parsley and serve.

    Note: For a flavorful variation, bits of cooked meat and sautéed mushrooms may be added to the rice mixture.
    Serves 8

The Cookbook Committee

Japanese, *Koshimaki,* early 18th cent., embroidered silk, 166.5 x 117 cm. Founders Society Purchase, with funds from Mr. and Mrs. George M. Endicott and Mr. and Mrs. Charles M. Endicott (81.909).

Barley Casserole

A savory grain and mushroom mixture —

1/2 cup butter
2 medium onions, chopped coarsely
3/4 pound mushrooms, sliced
1 1/2 cups pearl barley
3 pimentos, chopped coarsely
2 cups beef or chicken stock or bouillon
Salt and pepper to taste

Melt the butter in a saucepan and sauté the onions until golden. Add the mushrooms, stir for 1 minute, then add the barley, and cook over medium heat until the barley is delicately browned. Transfer the mixture to a casserole dish, add the pimentos and stock, salt and pepper to taste, cover, and bake in a 350°F. oven for 50–60 minutes or until the barley is tender and all of the liquid has been absorbed.

Serves 6–8

Judi Layton

Kitaōji Rosanjin, Japanese, 1883–1959, *Bowl with Design of Camellias,* stoneware with gold and overglaze enamels, h. 15.9 x diam. 36.2 cm. Founders Society Purchase, Acquisitions Fund (80.48).

Brown Rice and Lentils

Throughout history grains have constituted a necessary and much-revered staple. This mix of rice and lentils is a variation on one of civilization's oldest themes.

3/4 cup brown rice, rinsed and drained
3/4 cup lentils, rinsed and drained
4 cups water
2 teaspoons chicken stock base
1/2 teaspoon oregano
1/2 teaspoon basil
1/2 teaspoon onion salt
6 green onions, chopped

1 teaspoon salt
Pepper to taste

In a heavy pot with a tight-fitting lid, combine all of the ingredients, cover, and bring to a boil. Reduce the heat and simmer until the rice is tender and all of the liquid has been completely absorbed

(about 45 minutes). Serve the rice hot.

Note: Bits of cooked lamb may be added for a more substantial dish.

Serves 10

Marilyn F. Symmes

Old-fashioned Oats

For those nostalgic souls craving a taste of Americana, this historic recipe is a most healthy "picker-upper" in the morning!

3 cups water
1/2 teaspoon salt
1 1/3 cups old-fashioned oats
1/4 cup raisins
1/2 teaspoon cinnamon
1/4 teaspoon allspice
1/4 teaspoon nutmeg

1/4 teaspoon cloves
1 tablespoon raw sugar
Milk or half-and-half (optional)

In a large saucepan, combine the water and the salt, bring to a boil, and add the oats and raisins. Combine the spices and the sugar, add to the oatmeal, and sim-

mer for 25 minutes, stirring occasionally. Taste and add more sugar if necessary. Serve with milk or half-and-half.

Serves 2–4

The Honorable Jack Faxon

Sister Abigail's Blue Flower Omelette

Although the Shakers did not settle in Michigan, a few traveled to our state to cut timber in the western lower peninsula to be used in the making of their beautiful furniture. The timber was a fair exchange for the wholesome recipes they left behind.

4 eggs
4 tablespoons milk (or water)
Dash of salt and pepper
1 tablespoon parsley, minced
1 teaspoon chives, minced
2 tablespoons sweet butter
12 chive blossoms, washed

In a small bowl, lightly beat the eggs together with the milk, salt, pepper, parsley, and chives. In an omelette pan over medium heat, melt the butter, pour in the egg mixture, and leave undisturbed until the omelette begins to set. Lower the heat and, tipping the pan slightly, lift the edges of the omelette to let the uncooked egg mixture run underneath.

When the omelette is just firm, sprinkle the chive blossoms over the top, fold in half or in thirds, and serve immediately.
Serves 2–3

The Cookbook Committee

Rookwood Pottery, Decoration attributed to Hattie Horton, American, active 1882–84, *Jug*, 1883, clay, h. 11.9 cm. Gift of Mrs. Pearl Parker-Penick (79.185).

Helen Marin's Eggs Royale

Rich and creamy, this dish goes one better than Benedict.

½ pound Canadian bacon or ham
¾ cup condensed cream of mushroom soup
½ cup half-and-half
¼ cup butter
1½ dozen eggs
¼–⅓ pound sharp cheese, shredded or grated

Lightly brown the Canadian bacon (or ham cut into julienne strips) and use to line an 8-inch square glass baking dish;

set aside. Mix the soup with the half-and-half, blending well, and set aside. Melt the butter, add the eggs, scramble until they are soft, and let cool. Layer one-half of the eggs and one-half of the soup mixture over the bacon, repeating each layer once. Sprinkle the top with grated cheese and bake in a 350°F. oven for 30 minutes.
Serves 6

Helen Milliken

Hangover Eggs

They work!

1 tablespoon cider vinegar
1 tablespoon chili sauce
1 teaspoon Worcestershire sauce
Dollop of mustard
1 tablespoon butter
2 eggs

Preheat the oven to 325°F. Combine the cider vinegar, chili and Worcestershire sauces, mustard, and butter in a baking dish or ramekin and mix the ingredients together briefly over low heat. Drop the eggs in the center, place the dish in the oven, and bake for approximately 15 minutes, taking care not to overbake.
Serves 1

The Cookbook Committee

French Toast

Lafayette Park style, with a light and fluffy texture —

6–8 *pieces egg bread, sliced thickly*
12 *eggs*
1 *cup sugar*
2 *cups milk*
2 *tablespoons vanilla*
4–6 *cups oil for deep frying*
Michigan maple syrup (optional)
3 *teaspoons cinnamon combined with* 3
tablespoons sugar (optional)

Trim the crusts from the bread, slice each piece diagonally, and place on a jelly roll pan or cookie sheet with 1-inch sides. In a large bowl, combine the eggs, sugar, milk, and vanilla, pour the mixture over the bread slices, and place in the refrigerator for 30 minutes. Turn the slices and leave in the refrigerator overnight.

In a deep fryer, heat the oil to 350° F. Using a slotted spatula or tongs, fry a few pieces of bread at a time and remove to paper toweling to drain. Serve hot with Michigan maple syrup or a mixture of cinnamon and sugar sprinkled over the top.

Serves 3–4

Jackie Feigenson

Ansel Adams, American, 1902–1984, *Still Life, San Francisco, California*, ca. 1931, gelatin-silver print, 48.9 x 36.5 cm. John S. Newberry Fund (71.117).

James River Pancakes

A heavenly batter with lighter-than-air results —

2 eggs, separated
2 cups sour cream
2 cups flour
¼ teaspoon salt
2 teaspoons baking powder
1 teaspoon baking soda
4 tablespoons butter, softened
½ cup milk (approximately)
Michigan maple syrup or fresh blueberries
(optional)

In a large bowl, beat the egg yolks until light, add 1 cup of the sour cream, mix well, and set aside. Whip the egg whites until stiff but not dry and set aside.

Combine the dry ingredients and add to the egg yolk mixture alternately with the remaining sour cream, blending well. Add the butter and stir thoroughly. The batter should pour easily at this point (thin with a little milk if necessary). Gently fold in the beaten egg whites.

Heat a griddle and butter it lightly. Pour the batter to form 3-inch circles, turning them when bubbles appear on each pancake. Serve the hot pancakes smothered with Michigan maple syrup or fresh blueberries.

Serves 4

Bliss Clark

German Apple Pancake

Awake to the aroma of tart apples and cinnamon —

3 eggs
¾ cup milk
¾ cup flour
½ teaspoon salt
3–4 tart apples, peeled and sliced thinly
6 tablespoons butter
¼ cup sugar
1 teaspoon cinnamon
¼ teaspoon nutmeg

Preheat the oven to 450°F. Beat the eggs, milk, flour, and salt together until smooth and stir in ½ cup of the sliced apples. In a heavy, ovenproof, 10-inch skillet, melt 2 tablespoons of the butter and cook until bubbling. Pour the batter into the skillet, pushing the apples away from the sides of the pan. Place the skillet in the oven and bake for 15 minutes. Reduce the heat to 350°F. and continue baking for 5–10 minutes more. Remove the skillet from the oven and slide the pancake onto a platter; set aside and keep warm.

Melt the remaining butter in the same skillet. Stir in the sugar, cinnamon, and nutmeg, and bring the mixture to a boil. Stir in the remaining sliced apples, reduce the heat, and simmer for 10 minutes or until the apples are tender. Spoon the sauce into the center of the pancake and serve warm.

Serves 4

Joyce Tuck

Swiss Cheese Egg Scramble

The great short-notice mainstay for breakfast or brunch —

2 cups soft bread, trimmed and cubed
1¾ cups milk
8–10 eggs
½ teaspoon salt
⅛ teaspoon pepper
2 tablespoons butter
½ pound Swiss cheese, sliced
½ cup buttered bread crumbs
4–6 strips bacon, cooked and crumbled
(optional)

Combine the bread cubes with the milk and let stand for 5 minutes; drain and reserve the milk. Slightly beat the eggs and mix into the milk with the salt and pepper. In a skillet, melt the butter, add the egg mixture, and scramble until soft. Add the soaked bread cubes, mix well, and turn into a buttered, 9-inch square pan or a shallow casserole dish. Arrange the cheese slices over the top and sprinkle with the buttered bread crumbs. Bake at 400°F. for 10–15 minutes or until the cheese bubbles around the edges. Top with crumbled bacon and serve.

Note: This dish may be assembled ahead of time and refrigerated until needed (however, allow an additional 10 minutes baking time).

Serves 6–8

Martha Katz

Quiche Frittata

Non-stop flavor, Mediterranean style!

3 tablespoons oil
¾ cup green pepper, chopped
1½ cups mushrooms, sliced
1½ cups zucchini, sliced
¾ cup onion, chopped
1 large clove garlic, minced
6 eggs, beaten
¼ cup half-and-half
1 pound cream cheese, diced
1½ cups Cheddar cheese, shredded

2 cups white bread, cubed
1 teaspoon salt
¼ teaspoon pepper

Preheat the oven to 350°F. Grease two 8- or 9-inch springform pans and set aside. In a skillet, heat the oil and sauté the green pepper, mushrooms, zucchini, onion, and garlic until they are barely tender and let cool slightly. Beat the eggs with the half-and-half, add the cream cheese, Cheddar cheese, bread, salt, pepper, and sautéed vegetables, and mix well. Pour the mixture into the prepared pans and bake for 1 hour or until set. Cool the quiches for 10 minutes before serving.

Serves 10–12

Jan Miller

Quiche Magnifique

An openwork pattern of julienned vegetables adds the crowning glory —

4 ounces Swiss cheese, grated
1 tablespoon flour
2 tablespoons Parmesan cheese, grated
Pâte Brisée
    (baked pie shell; recipe follows)
2 tablespoons butter
1 leek or 1 small onion, chopped
1 cup sour cream or yogurt
4 eggs, beaten
1 teaspoon dill, basil, or thyme, chopped
¼ teaspoon salt
2–3 tomatoes, peeled, drained, and cut into
    strips
1 zucchini, cut into julienne strips

Preheat the oven to 350°F. Combine the Swiss cheese with the flour and the grated Parmesan and sprinkle over the bottom of the baked pie shell. In a sauté pan, melt the butter and sauté the leek. Transfer the leek to a bowl, combine with the sour cream, eggs, herbs, and salt, and pour over the cheeses in the shell. Arrange the tomatoes and zucchini over the top and bake for 40 minutes or until set. Let the quiche stand 10 minutes before serving.

Note: The quiche may be frozen after baking.

Serves 6

Pâte Brisée

1½ cups flour
½ cup butter
¼ teaspoon dill or thyme
½ teaspoon salt
1 egg yolk
4 tablespoons water
1 egg
1 tablespoon milk

Combine the flour, butter, dill or thyme, and salt in a food processor and process until the mixture resembles corn meal. Beat the egg yolk with the water, add to the dry ingredients, and process briefly or until the dough easily forms a ball. Press the dough in a flat circle and chill several hours or overnight.

Beat the whole egg with the milk and set aside. On a floured board, roll the chilled dough to fit a 12-inch flan pan, prick the shell, and chill. Preheat the oven to 400°F. Line the shell with foil, fill with weights or beans, and bake for 20–30 minutes. Remove the weights and the foil, brush the shell with the egg and milk mixture, and return to the oven for 6 minutes. Remove the shell and let cool.

Yields 1 12-inch pie or quiche shell

Joan Jacobs

Diego Rivera, *Woman with Grain* detail from *Detroit Industry/East Wall*, 1932/33, fresco, upper register side panel, 257.8 x 213.4 cm. Founders Society Purchase, Edsel B. Ford Fund and gift of Edsel B. Ford (33.10).

Greek (Attic), Attributed to the Group of Villa Giulia 3559, *Black-figured Band Cup*, ca. 530 B.C., ceramic, h. 30.5 x diam. 17.5 cm. Founders Society Purchase, Hill Memorial Fund (79.8).

White Stilton Mousse

Stilton takes its name from the parish of Stilton in Huntingdonshire, England, where it was originally made and marketed. Ranked among the world's great cheeses, it is rich, made of whole milk and cream, marbled with blue green veins, and has a crusty rind. This mousse is good for a luncheon accompanied by a crisp, green salad and fresh pears, or as a cheese course for a special dinner.

6 eggs
6 ounces Stilton cheese
Nutmeg to taste
1 small clove garlic, minced
Salt to taste
Dash of cayenne pepper
1 pint heavy cream

Place the eggs, cheese, nutmeg, garlic, salt, and cayenne pepper in a blender and process until smooth. Add the cream and process again until all of the ingredients are well blended. Pour the mixture into well-buttered individual ramekins or custard cups and sprinkle with a little additional nutmeg. Bake at 375°F. for 30 minutes or just until set. Unmold onto plates and serve hot.

Serves 6

Gayle Camden

Brazilian Palm Hearts Soufflé

Discover a delicate, gourmet flavor —

1 14-ounce can hearts of palm
¼ cup oil
1 small onion, chopped
¼ cup parsley, chopped
3 tablespoons flour
Salt and pepper to taste
3 eggs, separated

Preheat the oven to 350°F. Drain the palm hearts, reserve the liquid, cut the hearts vertically into 1-inch slices, and set aside. In a saucepan, heat the oil and sauté the onion and parsley, stir in the flour, salt, and pepper, and blend well. Gradually add the reserved liquid and stir until the mixture is smooth (add water if too thick). Remove the pan from the heat and set aside.

In a bowl, beat the egg yolks and slowly add the hot liquid, continuing to beat well. Beat the egg whites until stiff peaks form and fold into the yolk mixture. Add the palm hearts, mix thoroughly, and transfer to a 9-inch glass baking dish. Bake for approximately 30 minutes, remove from the oven, and serve immediately.

Serves 6

Marietta Boffi

Mushroom Spinach Strata

Lovely to look at and luscious to eat —

2 tablespoons butter
1 pound mushrooms, sliced
1 cup onion, chopped
8 slices firm white bread, trimmed and
    halved diagonally
1 cup Swiss cheese, shredded
1 10-ounce package frozen spinach, thawed,
    drained, and minced
3 eggs, beaten
2 cups milk
1 teaspoon salt
¼ teaspoon nutmeg
Pinch of black pepper

Grease a 10-inch quiche or pie pan and set aside. In a saucepan, melt the butter and sauté the mushrooms for about 5 minutes. Remove the mushrooms with a slotted spoon and set aside. Add the chopped onion to the pan, sauté for 5 minutes, and remove the pan from the heat.

Arrange six of the half-slices of bread to cover the bottom of the quiche pan. Atop the bread, spread a layer of three-quarters of the sautéed mushrooms, then add all of the onions, cheese, and spinach. Arrange eight of the half-slices of bread over the spinach, overlapping the pieces to fit in a circle, and place the remaining two half-slices over the center. In a bowl, combine the beaten eggs, milk, salt, nutmeg, and pepper and pour over the bread. Cover and refrigerate overnight.

Preheat the oven to 350°F. and bake the strata, uncovered, until it is almost firm (about 40 minutes). Place the remaining mushrooms in the center of the strata and bake 10–15 minutes more or until a knife inserted in the center comes out clean.

Serves 6

Jackie Eckhous

Spinach-filled Cheese Soufflé

Appetites sharpen when this appears on the table.

⅓ cup plus 2 tablespoons butter
1 medium onion, chopped
2 10-ounce packages frozen spinach, cooked
    and drained
1 teaspoon salt
Dash of nutmeg
¼ cup plus 2 tablespoons Parmesan cheese,
    grated
½ cup sour cream
6 tablespoons flour
Dash of cayenne pepper
1¼ cups milk
¾ cup Cheddar cheese, grated
7 eggs, separated
¼ teaspoon cream of tartar
Tomato Sauce (optional)
    (see recipe p. 119)

Preheat the oven to 350°F. In a skillet, melt 2 tablespoons of the butter, sauté the onion until transparent, transfer to a blender or food processor, and add the spinach, ¼ teaspoon salt, nutmeg, ¼ cup Parmesan, and sour cream. Process until all of the ingredients are well blended and set aside.*

Grease a jelly roll pan, line with waxed paper, grease the paper, and set aside. In a saucepan, melt the remaining butter, stir in the flour, cayenne, and ¾ teaspoon of the salt. Using a whisk, stir in the milk and ½ cup of the Cheddar. Cook and stir until thickened.

Beat the egg yolks and add to the cheese mixture. Beat the egg whites with the cream of tartar until stiff peaks form, then fold into the cheese and eggs. Spread the mixture over the greased paper in the jelly roll pan and bake for 15 minutes or until set. Cut another piece of waxed paper the length of the jelly roll pan and evenly sprinkle with the remaining Parmesan. Loosen the edges of the soufflé and turn it out onto the paper. Spread the soufflé with the reserved filling and roll up lengthwise. Return it to the jelly roll pan, cover the top with the remaining Cheddar, and place it under the broiler until the cheese melts and browns lightly. Slice the roll diagonally and, if desired, serve with a mushroom or tomato sauce.

*May be prepared in advance to this point.

Serves 6–8

Eleanor Sugarman

VEGETABLES AND LEGUMES

*T*oo often included in meals solely as a concession to nutrition and not for their variety of color, texture, and flavor, vegetables and legumes are hereby given the attention they deserve. These exciting recipes may be prepared and served as tradition demands, to complement an entrée, or they may be enjoyed as delicious meatless meals in their own right.

Vegetable, fruit, and flower forms are among the motifs used to decorate the *Covered Vegetable Dish,* which is one of a pair of elaborate silver serving dishes modeled by English artist Paul Storr. Many artists have used vegetables and fruits as subjects in their art, delighting in the challenge of depicting their various shapes, colors, and textures. Gourds, with their unusual variations in color, smooth or bumpy skins, and amusing shapes have intrigued artists through the ages, as evidenced by the Peruvian *Vessel in Form of a Squash with Spout and Handle* fashioned ca. 1200-1470 the *Ewer in Double Gourd Shape* made in early twelfth-century Korea, and the painting *Preparations for a Meal* by seventeenth-century artist Abraham Hendricksz. van Beyeren.

Abraham Hendricksz. van Beyeren, Dutch, 1620/21-ca. 1690, *Preparations for a Meal* (detail), 1664, oil on canvas, 80.6 x 68.6 cm. Founders Society Purchase (35.21).

Brandied Carrots

A spirited dish —

Salt to taste
Water
1½ pounds carrots, cut into pieces
¼ cup butter
¼ teaspoon pepper

2 tablespoons cream
1 tablespoon brandy

In salted water, cook the carrots until tender, drain, and purée in batches in a food processor. Add the butter, addi-tional salt if desired, pepper, cream, and brandy and process until well blended. Taste and correct the seasonings. Reheat and serve immediately.
Serves 4

Janet Johnson

Celery Side Dish

Simple, but succulent —

1 cup celery, cut into 1-inch pieces
1 tablespoon onion, minced
2 tablespoons butter
⅛ teaspoon each salt and pepper

Combine all of the ingredients in a saucepan, cover, and cook over low heat for 15 minutes. Shake the pan several times during cooking but do not un-cover to stir. The celery should be slightly crisp when done.
Note: A 10-ounce package of frozen peas with 1 tablespoon of chopped mint may be substituted as an interesting vari-ation to the celery.
Serves 2

Clara Janigian

Brussels Sprouts in Cream

A blanket of cream sauce brings out the special flavor.

1 pint Brussels sprouts, washed and trimmed
Water
Salt to taste
1 cup cream
1 teaspoon curry powder
Pepper to taste

Cut a cross in the stem end of each sprout, place in a saucepan, cover with boiling, salted water, and cook until tender. Drain the sprouts in a colander, run cold water over them to preserve their bright green color, drain, and chop finely. Return the sprouts to the pan, add the cream and curry powder, bring to a boil, and cook until the cream thickens and is almost completely absorbed. Add salt and pepper to taste and serve.
Serves 5–6

The Cookbook Committee

Asparagus Royale

The most elegant of vegetables —

Water
4 pounds asparagus, washed and trimmed
6 egg yolks, beaten lightly
1 cup sour cream
½ teaspoon salt
⅛ teaspoon white pepper

1 tablespoon lemon juice
2 tablespoons fresh chives, chopped finely

In water to cover, cook the asparagus just until tender (about 5–8 minutes), drain, and keep warm. In a saucepan over low heat, combine the egg yolks, sour cream, salt, and pepper. Cook for 2–4 minutes, whisking constantly, until thoroughly heated. Remove the pan from the heat, stir in the lemon juice and chives, and mix well. Pour the sauce over the aspara-gus and serve immediately.
Serves 8

Joyce Tuck

Peruvian (Chimu), *Vessel in Form of a Squash with Spout and Handle*, ca. 1200–1470, ceramic, 17.1 x 13.3 x 19.7 cm. Founders Society Purchase, Clarence E. Wilcox Fund (71.13).

Broccoli Casserole

A mealtime favorite —

4 tablespoons cornflake crumbs
1½ tablespoons butter, melted
1½ tablespoons flour
½ cup milk
¾ cup mayonnaise
1 tablespoon dried onion flakes
3 eggs, beaten well
⅛ teaspoon salt
⅛ teaspoon pepper
2 10-ounce packages frozen, chopped
   broccoli, cooked

Preheat the oven to 350°F. Sprinkle 2 tablespoons of the crumbs over the bottom of a greased 8- by 8-inch pan, add the butter and flour, and stir until smooth. Place the pan over low heat, add the milk, mayonnaise, onion flakes, eggs, salt, and pepper, and blend well. Fold in the broccoli, sprinkle the remaining crumbs over the top, and bake uncovered for 30–40 minutes.

Serves 6–8

Nettie Weinberg

Cauliflower-Tomato Scallop

The secret's in the marriage of these fresh vegetables.

1 large head cauliflower, broken into
   flowerets
Water
6 tablespoons butter
½ cup celery, chopped
¼ cup onion, chopped finely
¼ cup green pepper, chopped finely
¾ teaspoon salt
¼ teaspoon pepper
¼ cup flour
2 cups milk
1½ cups Cheddar cheese, shredded

3 large, firm, ripe tomatoes, sliced
½ cup fine, dry bread crumbs

Preheat the oven to 400°F. Cook the cauliflower, covered, in 1 inch of boiling, salted water for about 5 minutes, drain, and set aside. In a saucepan, melt the butter, add the celery, onion, and green pepper, and cook until tender. Blend in the salt, pepper, and flour, add the milk, and cook over low heat, stirring constantly until thickened. Add the cheese,

stir until melted, and remove the pan from the heat.

Arrange a layer of cauliflower in a casserole, cover with a small amount of the cheese sauce, then arrange a layer of the sliced tomatoes, and cover with a little more sauce. Top with the remaining cauliflower and sauce, sprinkle with the bread crumbs, and bake for 20–25 minutes or until lightly browned.

Serves 6

Lucie Kelly

Broccoli-Sauerkraut Casserole

Hollandaise provides the tartly elegant topping for this unusual combination.

2 bunches fresh broccoli (or 2 10-ounce
   packages frozen broccoli)
1 16-ounce can sauerkraut, drained
   partially
2 tablespoons butter
Lemon juice to taste

Salt and pepper to taste
2 cups Hollandaise sauce

Preheat the oven to 350°F. Cook the broccoli just until tender and set aside. In a baking dish, place a layer of sauerkraut and then a layer of broccoli, add a little of the butter, season with lemon

juice, salt, and pepper, and repeat the process once more. Bake for 30 minutes and garnish with Hollandaise sauce before serving.

Serves 8

Margot Kessler

Paul Storr, English, 1771-1844, *Covered Vegetable Dish* (one of a pair), 1816, silver, 20.3 x 36.5 x 27 cm. Gift of Dr. and Mrs. Arthur R. Bloom (71.298).

Irish Potato Crisps

Our favorite chips, Celtic style!

6 baking potatoes, scrubbed but left
    unpeeled
Seasoned salt

Preheat the oven to 500°F. Cut the potatoes lengthwise into strips ½-inch wide by ⅛-inch thick. Place the strips on a greased baking sheet, sprinkle with the seasoned salt, and bake for a few minutes or until the potatoes puff up and are lightly browned. Serve in lieu of bread or as hors d'oeuvres.
    Serves 6

The Cookbook Committee

Cabbage Casserole

A tasty revelation —

Water
3 cups cabbage, shredded finely
1½ cups canned stewed tomatoes
    (reserve liquid)
¼ teaspoon paprika
½ teaspoon salt
2 teaspoons brown sugar
⅔ cup dry bread crumbs
¾ cup Cheddar cheese, shredded

Preheat the oven to 325°F. In a small amount of water, cook the cabbage for 5 minutes, drain, and set aside. Combine the tomatoes (with liquid), seasonings, and brown sugar and set aside. Mix together the crumbs and the cheese and set aside.

Layer the vegetables in a buttered baking dish (beginning with the tomatoes), sprinkling each layer and the top of the casserole with a little of the cheese mixture. Bake for about 30 minutes or until the casserole bubbles and the top is browned.
    Serves 6

Natalie Lederer

Eggplant Creole

Uniquely flavored to bring you a bit of Old New Orleans —

1 medium eggplant, peeled and diced
Water
3 tablespoons butter
3 tablespoons flour
3 large tomatoes, diced
1 green pepper, chopped
1 small onion, chopped
1 teaspoon salt
1 tablespoon brown sugar
1 bay leaf
2 whole cloves

Bread crumbs
Sharp Cheddar cheese, grated

Preheat the oven to 350°F. Cook the eggplant for 10 minutes in boiling, salted water, drain, and place in a greased, 3-quart casserole. Melt the butter, add the flour, and stir until well blended. Add the remaining vegetables to the butter mixture along with the salt, brown sugar, bay leaf, and cloves and cook for 5 min-

utes. Pour the vegetables over the eggplant, cover with the bread crumbs and grated cheese, and bake for about 30 minutes or until bubbly.
    Note: The addition of ground beef to this side dish creates a special entrée.
    Serves 6

Betty Bird

Crispy Eggplant

An easy dish to prepare in advance —

1 eggplant, peeled
⅓ cup mayonnaise
2 tablespoons instant dried onions
⅓ cup fine, dry bread crumbs
⅓ cup Parmesan cheese, grated
1 teaspoon Italian herb seasoning

Preheat the oven to 425°F. Slice the eggplant horizontally into ½-inch thick pieces and set aside. Combine the mayonnaise and onions and set aside. Mix together the crumbs, cheese, and Italian herb seasoning and spread over the bottom of a shallow dish. Spread both sides of each eggplant slice with the mayonnaise and onion mixture, coat with the crumbs, and place in a shallow baking dish or pan large enough to accommodate the eggplant in one layer. Bake for 20–30 minutes and serve.

Serves 4–6

Bea Wells

Creamed Cauliflower and Peas

A dash of nutmeg does the trick.

1 large head cauliflower, broken into
    flowerets
¼ cup water
¼ teaspoon salt
1 10-ounce package frozen peas
Milk
¾ cup onion, chopped finely
6 tablespoons butter
3 tablespoons flour
¼ teaspoon pepper
¼ teaspoon nutmeg
1 cup light cream or half-and-half
½ cup dry bread crumbs

Preheat the oven to 400°F. Cook the cauliflower until barely tender and drain. In a saucepan, bring the water and salt to a boil, add the peas, simmer for 5 minutes, and drain the liquid into a large measuring cup. Add enough milk to the liquid to make 2 cups and set aside.

In a separate pan, sauté the onions in 4 tablespoons of the butter, stir in the flour, pepper, and nutmeg, and blend well. Gradually stir in the reserved liquid and add the cream, stirring constantly. Combine the cauliflower, peas, and onion mixture in a 2-quart casserole. Melt the remaining butter, mix with the bread crumbs, and sprinkle over the top.* Cover the casserole, bake for 20 minutes, uncover, and bake until bubbly.

At this point, the casserole may be covered and stored in the refrigerator for up to 24 hours.

Serves 6–8

Arden Poole

Spinach Timbales

A rich symphony of flavors —

2 tablespoons butter
2 tablespoons flour
1 cup milk
3 eggs, beaten
½ cup Cheddar cheese, grated
¼ cup chicken stock
Cayenne pepper
Salt
Pepper
2 10-ounce packages frozen, chopped
    spinach, cooked and drained well

Preheat the oven to 325°F. In a saucepan over low heat, melt the butter, stir in the flour and milk, and cook until thickened. Add the eggs, cheese, chicken stock, and seasonings, stir to blend, and add to the spinach.

Butter 8 ½-cup timbale molds and cut pieces of waxed paper to fit over the bottom of each mold. Fill the molds to the top with the spinach mixture, place them in a large pan, and surround with hot water to one-half the depth of the molds. Bake for 1 hour, remove from the oven, and turn the timbales out onto a platter. Remove the waxed paper and serve with a rich-bodied mushroom sauce.

Serves 8

Gaylord W. Gillis

Potatoes Parmesan

Ah, simplicity!

6 baking potatoes, scrubbed and peeled
Cold water
¼ cup flour
¼ cup Parmesan cheese
¾ teaspoon salt
⅛ teaspoon pepper
⅓ cup butter

Preheat the oven to 375°F. Cut the potatoes lengthwise into six sections each, let stand in a bowl of cold water until needed, and then drain thoroughly. Combine the flour, cheese, salt, and pepper in a paper bag, add a few of the moist potatoes at a time, and shake to coat. Melt the butter in a jelly roll pan, spread the potato slices in the pan, and roll in the butter to coat all sides. Bake for approximately 1 hour.

Serves 6

The Cookbook Committee

Indian Fried Tomatoes

Excellent alone or as a complement to curry dishes —

4 ripe tomatoes
2 tablespoons butter
Salt and pepper
Dill
Turmeric
4 teaspoons dry sherry
Parsley

Cut the top and bottom from each tomato and discard. In a very large frying pan over medium to high heat, melt the butter and fry the tomatoes on both sides. Sprinkle each side with salt, pepper, dill, and turmeric. When the tomatoes just begin to collapse, remove them to a serving dish. Add the sherry to the cooking juices in the pan, bring to a full boil, and cook for 1 minute. Pour the sherry sauce over the tomatoes and garnish with parsley.

Serves 4

Roberta Van Horn

Leeks and Root Vegetables in Cheese Sauce

Brings below-the-earth bounty to the table —

Water
4 large leeks, sliced thinly
1 pound parsnips or turnips (or a
    combination), peeled and sliced thinly
5 tablespoons butter
4 tablespoons flour
1 cup milk
1 chicken bouillon cube
Few shakes of seasoned salt
Pepper to taste
5 ounces Swiss cheese, cubed
Parmesan cheese, grated

Preheat the oven to 350°F. In a large saucepan with water to cover, cook the vegetables until barely tender. Drain and reserve the cooking liquid and set the vegetables aside.

Melt 4 tablespoons of the butter, add the flour, and stir until smooth. Add the milk, 1½ cups of the vegetable cooking juices, and the bouillon and let simmer until thickened. Season with seasoned salt and pepper and blend with the vegetables.

Transfer the vegetables to a shallow baking dish and spread the cubes of cheese over the top. Pour the sauce over all, covering completely, and sprinkle with the Parmesan. Dot with the remaining tablespoon of butter and bake for 30 minutes. Place under the broiler briefly to brown.

Note: The sauce is also excellent with a combination of leeks and cauliflower.

Serves 8

Irma E. Stevens

Jean François de Troy, French, 1679-1752, *The Country Lunch* (detail), 1724/25, oil on canvas, 224.1 x 165.1 cm. Founders Society Purchase in memory of Eleanor Clay Ford; Benson and Edith Ford Fund, Henry Ford II Fund, Mr. and Mrs. Walter Buhl Ford II Fund, William and Martha Ford Fund, Elizabeth, Allan and Warren Shelden Fund, Macauley Fund, Edsel and Eleanor Ford Fund and New Endowment Fund (77.72).

Red Fox Inn Tomato Pudding

An old-fashioned offering from the inn near Ernest Hemingway's Michigan summer home —

1 12-ounce can tomatoes, drained
½ cup dark brown sugar, packed firmly
¼ cup butter, melted
¼ teaspoon salt
1 cup dry white bread, cut into 1-inch squares

In a saucepan over low heat, combine the tomatoes, sugar, butter, salt, and bread and cook for 2½ hours, stirring frequently and watching carefully to avoid burning.

Note: The pudding may be made in advance and reheated, uncovered, for 20–30 minutes in an oven preheated to 375°F.

Serves 3–4

Trudi Wineman

Riverton Squash Casserole

The golden light of summer fills this dish.

4 cups yellow summer squash, sliced
1 cup onion, chopped
1 cup green pepper, chopped
¼ cup butter, softened to room temperature
½ cup saltines, crushed coarsely
2 eggs, beaten lightly

Salt and pepper
½ cup Cheddar cheese, grated

Preheat the oven to 375°F. In a steamer, combine the squash, onion, and green pepper and steam for 10 minutes or until tender. Place the vegetables in a bowl, stir in the butter and saltines, and let stand to cool. Stir in the eggs, salt, and pepper and transfer the mixture to a buttered, 1-quart baking dish. Sprinkle with the cheese and bake for 30–45 minutes.

Serves 4–6

Larry Devine

Stuffed Zucchini

A zesty tomato sauce tops this dish.

4 zucchini (each approximately 5–6 inches long)
6 small green onions (white portion only), chopped finely
2 tablespoons butter
⅓ pound mushrooms (caps and stems)
½ cup spinach, cooked, squeezed dry, and chopped finely (or enough to make 1 generous cup when combined with the mushrooms and onions)
Tomato Sauce (recipe follows)
½ cup fresh Parmesan cheese, grated

Preheat the oven to 350°F. Split the zucchini lengthwise and remove the seedy pulp with a spoon. Steam the zucchini for 2–4 minutes and set aside.

In a saucepan, sauté the onions in the butter until soft, add the mushrooms, and cook until all of the liquid has evaporated. Add the spinach and salt and pepper to taste. Arrange the zucchini in a buttered baking dish, fill the center of each with the spinach mixture, and neatly top the spinach with the tomato sauce. Sprinkle with the Parmesan and bake for 10–15 minutes.

Serves 6–8

Tomato Sauce

2 teaspoons onion, chopped
Butter
4½ ounces tomato paste
½ cup heavy cream
¼ teaspoon dried basil, crushed or ground with a mortar and pestle

In a small saucepan, sauté the onion in the butter, add the remaining ingredients, and stir to blend well.

Yields ½–¾ cup

Bishie Beatty

Stuffed Warm Avocados

Wonderful on their own or in a supporting role —

1/4 cup olive oil
2 tablespoons scallions, chopped
1 16-ounce can whole tomatoes, drained
    and chopped (or 1 1/4 cups fresh
    tomatoes)
4 tablespoons seasoned stuffing mix
1/4 cup Parmesan cheese, grated
3 large avocados, halved and seeded but not
    peeled
Butter

1/2 teaspoon salt
White pepper

Heat the oil in a skillet, add the scallions, and cook until wilted. Add the tomatoes and simmer for 5 minutes. Add 2 tablespoons of the stuffing mix and stir to blend; keep hot but take care not to burn. Combine the remaining stuffing mix and the cheese and set aside.

Brush the cut sides of the avocados with butter and season with salt and pepper. Fill the cavities with the hot tomato mixture and sprinkle with the reserved stuffing mix. Broil approximately 4 inches from the flame until browned (2–3 minutes) and serve immediately.
    Serves 6

The Cookbook Committee

Skillet Cabbage

An aromatic accompaniment to a winter's meal —

3 tablespoons butter (may be combined with
    bacon fat)
1 onion, chopped
2 carrots, grated
3 stalks celery, sliced
1/2 head cabbage, shredded
1/2 green pepper, diced
1/2 teaspoon sugar
1 teaspoon chicken stock base
1/4 cup water
Salt and pepper to taste
3 slices bacon, cooked and crumbled
    (optional)

In a saucepan, melt the butter and sauté the onion, carrots, and celery for a few minutes or until the onion is soft. Add the cabbage, green pepper, sugar, chicken stock base, and water, cover, and simmer until the vegetables are tender (about 10 minutes). Season with salt and pepper and garnish with the crumbled bacon.
    Serves 5–6

The Cookbook Committee

Spinach Casserole

A mélange of flavors and textures —

4 ounces cream cheese
1/4 cup butter
2 10-ounce packages frozen, chopped
    spinach, cooked and drained well
7 ounces canned artichoke hearts, sliced
4 ounces canned water chestnuts, sliced

Preheat the oven to 350°F. In a saucepan, melt the cheese and butter, add the spinach, and blend well. Add the artichoke hearts and water chestnuts, stir, and pour into a greased casserole dish. Bake for 20 minutes or until the mixture is bubbly.
    Serves 8

Frances Goldberg

Korean, *Ewer in Double Gourd Shape*, Koryŏ Dynasty, early 12th cent., celadon-glazed black ware with inlaid decoration, h. 21.8 x diam. 14 cm. Founders Society Purchase, with funds from Mr. and Mrs. Charles M. Endicott (1983.4).

FRESHWATER FISH
AND SEAFOOD

*R*egarded as a dietary staple by those who dwell along coasts and water-ways and as a luxury by many inland peoples, fish and seafood constitute a major source of nutrition as well as offering a range of delicate flavors, colors, forms, and textures to delight the eye and the palate.

The importance of fish in many cultures is reflected in art works such as the *Fish Effigy Vessel,* fashioned by a Chimu artisan of Peru ca. 1200–1470, or the handscroll *Fisherman and Poem* by Guo Xu, a Chinese artist of the Ming Dynasty. *Trout,* a contemporary lithograph by American artist Jack Beal, demonstrates with clear colors and sharp detail a great enthusiasm for the sport of trout fishing.

Similar to the glistening catch shown in William Merritt Chase's *Yield of the Waters* is the abundant variety of fish yielded by Michigan's lakes and streams. Both simple and elaborate methods of preparing freshwater fish, such as whitefish and salmon, and mouth-watering seafood dishes are included in the tempting "catches" offered here.

William Merritt Chase, American, 1849-1916, *The Yield of the Waters* (detail), 1878 (altered ca. 1890), oil on canvas, 124.5 x 165.1 cm. City of Detroit Purchase (16.5).

Baked Michigan Whitefish

A sumptuous presentation of a native delicacy —

3 pounds fillet of whitefish
Salt and pepper to taste
2 cups sour cream
½ pound mushrooms, chopped
2 tablespoons butter, melted
Paprika to taste

Wash the fish fillet, pat dry, and place skin side down in a buttered baking dish. Season the fillet with salt and pepper and cover completely with the sour cream. Sauté the mushrooms in the melted butter, spread over the top of the fish, and dust with paprika. Bake in a 350°F. oven for approximately 40 minutes. The fish should flake easily when done.

Serves 6

Annette Levin

Fish in Béchamel Sauce

Smooth and spirited flavor —

1 pound firm fish such as haddock, halibut, or scrod
White wine
Water
Salt and pepper to taste
4–6 tablespoons butter
2 eggs, hard-boiled and sliced
2 tablespoons flour
¾ cup milk
¾ cup heavy cream
Seasoned salt to taste
Herbed bread crumbs

Preheat the oven to 350°F. Place the fish in a skillet and add a half-and-half mixture of white wine and water to cover. Add salt and pepper to taste and simmer the fish gently for about 15 minutes or until it flakes easily; drain and remove the skin and bones. Place the fish in a shallow, buttered baking dish and top with a layer of the sliced, hard-boiled eggs.

In a saucepan, melt 2 tablespoons of the butter, add the flour, and stir until well blended. Add the milk and cream and cook over low heat until thickened. Season the sauce with seasoned salt and pour over the fish. Cover with the herbed bread crumbs, dot with the remaining butter, and bake for 20–30 minutes or until the sauce bubbles.

Serves 4

Betsy Campbell

Broiled Scallops

As an entrée or hors d'oeuvres, they're simply delicious!

½ cup butter
2 tablespoons scallions, chopped finely
2 cloves garlic, minced
½ teaspoon sweet basil
½ teaspoon tarragon
2 tablespoons parsley, minced
½ teaspoon salt
Dash of freshly ground pepper
2 tablespoons cornflake crumbs
2 pounds bay scallops, rinsed and drained
1–2 lemons, quartered

Melt the butter in a skillet and add the scallions, garlic, basil, tarragon, parsley, salt, and pepper. Sauté the mixture over low heat for 2 minutes. Add the cornflake crumbs and cook 1 minute longer. Arrange the scallops in a flat, shallow, baking dish and cover with the butter mixture, coating thoroughly. Broil the scallops approximately 4 inches from the flame for about 8 minutes, turning them occasionally to brown on both sides. Serve the scallops garnished with the lemon wedges.

Note: Rather than broiling, the scallops may be added to the skillet containing the butter mixture and sautéed quickly until they are a golden brown.

Serves 4 as an entrée (or 8 as an hors d'oeuvres)

Mary Ann Simon

Charles Robert Ashbee, English, 1863–1942, *Double Loop-handled Bowl*, 1904/05, silver, 6.3 x 24.7 cm. Founders Society Purchase, Robert H. Tannahill Foundation Fund (81.912).

Friskie Fish with Herbs

A fail-safe method of cooking ideal for most fish —

3 pounds lake trout, salmon, or whitefish, butterflied and boned
Salt and pepper to taste
2 scallions, chopped
1 lemon, sliced
4 sprigs fresh parsley, chopped
4 sprigs fresh dill, chopped
4 sprigs fresh tarragon, chopped
1 lemon, quartered

Rinse the fish and pat dry. Sprinkle the cavity with salt and pepper and fill with the scallions, lemon slices, parsley, dill, and tarragon, reserving a portion of the herbs to sprinkle over the top. Place the fish in a baking pan and cover tightly with aluminum foil. Bake at 375°F. for 40 minutes to 1 hour; the fish should flake easily when done. Carefully remove the fish to a platter and garnish with the lemon wedges and another sprig or two of parsley.

Serves 6–8

Mary Page Hickey

Finnan Haddie

A popular dish, this recipe was originally called Findhorn Haddock after the Scottish fishing port of Findhorn where it was first prepared. It will add a bracing Scottish air to your brunch.

2 pounds finnan haddie (smoked haddock)
Water
4 tablespoons butter
3 tablespoons flour
2 cups milk
Nutmeg and pepper to taste
Parmesan cheese, grated

Place the finnan haddie in a pan with water to cover. Cover the pan, bring to a boil, reduce the heat, and simmer for 15 minutes or until the fish flakes easily. Drain, set aside to cool, then flake the fish into large pieces, removing any bones, and place in a shallow, 1½-quart casserole.

In a saucepan, melt the butter and combine with the flour and milk to make a cream sauce. Season the sauce with the nutmeg and pepper (but no salt), and pour over the fish. Sprinkle the finnan haddie with grated Parmesan, bake for 30 minutes at 350°F., place briefly under the broiler to brown, and serve immediately.

Note: As a variation, chopped, hard-boiled egg may be layered over the fish before the cream sauce is added.

Serves 4–5

Margie Gillis

Whitefish Farci

Filled with the mouth-watering combination of oysters and shrimp —

4–6 pounds fresh whitefish, red snapper, or
    trout, butterflied and boned
1 teaspoon seasoned salt
1 tablespoon Worcestershire sauce
6 tablespoons butter
1 large onion, chopped
1 stalk celery, chopped
1 teaspoon salt
¼ teaspoon pepper
¾ pound shrimp, cooked
½ pound mushrooms, sliced
1 tablespoon parsley
1 pint fresh oysters, with liquid
    (or ½ cup white wine)
¾ cup bread crumbs
1 cup sherry

Rinse the fish in cold water, pat dry, and season inside and out with the seasoned salt and the Worcestershire sauce. Place the fish in a greased, foil-lined broiler pan and set aside.

In a skillet, melt 4 tablespoons of the butter, sauté the onion and celery until golden, and season with the salt and pepper. Add the shrimp, mushrooms, and parsley, and sauté briefly. Drain the oysters and add the oyster liquid and the bread crumbs to the skillet, stirring well. Stuff the fish loosely with the shrimp and mushroom mixture and close, securing with skewers and string or sewing with a heavy needle and thread.

Melt the remaining 2 tablespoons of butter and brush over the fish. Pour one-half of the sherry over the fish and bake in a 400°F. oven for approximately 45 minutes or until the fish flakes easily; add the oysters and the remaining sherry in the last 5 minutes of baking time. Remove the skewers and the string and slice to serve.

Note: The stuffing may be varied by omitting the shrimp or by using a combination of mushrooms, onion, and frozen spinach soufflé.

Serves 8

Alice Jean Gottesman

Iranian, *Chalice with Painted Decoration of Birds*, Sialk III Period, ca. 4000–3000 B.C., earthenware, h. 14.6 x diam. 7.6 cm. City of Detroit Purchase (30.449).

Pickled Fish with Almonds

A wonderful dish for a buffet or summer brunch, it's also a boon when unexpected guests arrive — with refrigeration, it keeps for up to two weeks.

5 pounds trout, cut into 1½- to 2-inch slices
1 pound pickerel, cut into 1½- to 2-inch
    slices
4–6 cups white vinegar
3 large onions, sliced
2 stalks celery (with leaves)
6 bay leaves
12 whole allspice
1 tablespoon salt
2 quarts cold water
1 cup sugar
3 lemons, sliced thinly
1 cup blanched almonds

Arrange the fish in a shallow dish with a lid, add enough of the vinegar to cover, and marinate overnight.

Combine the onion, celery, and spices, add the cold water, and bring to a boil. Reduce the heat and simmer for 20 minutes. Strain the stock into a large soup pot and discard the vegetables. Add the sugar and 2 cups of vinegar to the stock. Remove the fish from the marinade, place gently in the stock, and cover. Bring to a simmer over medium heat, reduce the heat, uncover, and cook for 20 minutes. Remove the fish from the stock pot and layer gently with the sliced lemons and almonds in a crock or other heavy dish. Cover and chill in the refrigerator for two days or more before serving.

Serves 10

Sylvia Dunitz

Scalloped Oysters

Unsurpassed as a main course, it's also a great complement to ham or poultry.

1 cup cracker crumbs
½ cup seasoned bread crumbs
½ cup butter, melted
1 pint oysters
¼ teaspoon salt
½ teaspoon pepper
4 tablespoons oyster liquid
2 tablespoons light cream

Combine the cracker crumbs, bread crumbs, and butter and spread approximately one-third of the mixture in a thin layer in the bottom of a 1-quart, shallow, buttered baking dish. Drain the oysters and reserve 4 tablespoons of the liquid. Spread the oysters over the crumbs and sprinkle with salt and pepper. Drizzle one-half of the reserved oyster liquid and one-half of the cream over the oysters. Repeat the layers of crumbs, oysters, and liquids, topping with a final layer of crumbs. (There should be no more than two layers of oysters; three or more layers will result in the middle layers being underdone.) Bake in a 450°F. oven for 30 minutes.

Note: For a zestier flavor, substitute crushed seasoned croutons for the cracker crumbs.

Serves 5–6

Alfred and Doris Pelham

Fillet of Sole en Timbales

Guests will love the delicate balance of flavors of the sole and the crab.

Juice of ½ lemon
4 fillets of sole, halved lengthwise
Salt and pepper to taste
6 tablespoons butter
1 tablespoon onion, minced
1 tablespoon celery, chopped
1 tablespoon parsley, chopped
½ cup saltine cracker crumbs
½ pound crabmeat or salmon, rinsed, drained, and flaked
1 egg
Sauce Velouté
(recipe follows)
16 shrimp, cooked
Fresh dill

Preheat the oven to 375°F. Squeeze the lemon juice over both sides of the sole and pat dry. Score the sides of the fish 2 or 3 times and season with salt and pepper. Butter an 8-cup muffin tin or four 6-ounce ramekins. Coil each fillet, dark side in with the ends overlapping, and place each in a muffin cup.

In a skillet, melt 2 tablespoons of the butter and sauté the onion, celery, and parsley until tender (about 5 minutes). Add the cracker crumbs, flaked crabmeat, and egg, mix well, and season to taste. Spoon the crabmeat mixture into the center of the coiled fillets. Melt the remaining butter, brush the fillets and crabmeat, and bake for 15 minutes. Using two spoons, carefully lift each timbale from the tin onto a platter. Cover with *Sauce Velouté* and garnish with the cooked shrimp and fresh sprigs of dill.

Serves 4

Sauce Velouté

3 tablespoons butter
¼ cup onion, minced
3 tablespoons flour
1 cup heavy cream
¼ cup dry white wine
¼ cup chicken stock
½ cup clam juice
Salt and pepper to taste
Lemon juice to taste
Cayenne pepper to taste

In a heavy saucepan, melt the butter and sauté the onions until soft. Add the flour, whisk to blend, and cook several minutes (but do not let the flour brown). Stir in the cream, wine, chicken stock, and clam juice. Simmer, stirring constantly, until the mixture thickens (about 5 minutes). Season the sauce with salt, pepper, lemon juice, and cayenne pepper to taste.

Note: The sauce may be made in advance but must be stored with plastic wrap covering the surface so that a skin does not form.

Yields 2 cups

Jane Solomon

Fillet of Flounder Farci

Fruits of the sea yield a captivating flavor —

7 tablespoons butter
¼ cup shallots or onions, chopped
¼ pound mushrooms, chopped
4 ounces small shrimp, cooked
4 ounces cooked crab, chopped
½ cup cracker crumbs
2 tablespoons fresh parsley, chopped
Salt and pepper to taste
2 pounds fillet of flounder
2 tablespoons flour
1 cup dry vermouth
1 bay leaf
4 peppercorns
¾ cup half-and-half
1 egg yolk
4 ounces Gruyère cheese, grated
Paprika to taste

Preheat the oven to 350°F. Melt 4 tablespoons of the butter in a skillet and sauté the shallots until golden. Add the mushrooms, toss quickly, and then add the shrimp, crab, cracker crumbs, parsley, salt, and pepper and mix well. Place a well-rounded tablespoon of the stuffing on each fillet, roll up, and secure with toothpicks. Place the stuffed fillets seam side down in a shallow baking dish.

Melt the remaining 3 tablespoons of butter in a medium-sized skillet, add the flour, mix quickly to make a roux, and set aside. In a small pan, combine the vermouth, bay leaf, and peppercorns, bring to a boil, and simmer for 5 minutes. Strain the mixture, add to the roux, and cook until the mixture thickens. Combine the half-and-half with the egg yolk and add to the vermouth mixture, blending thoroughly.

Pour the sauce over the fillets, cover with foil, and bake for 20 minutes. Remove the foil, sprinkle the flounder with the Gruyère, and dust with the paprika. Bake the fish uncovered for 5–10 minutes or until the cheese melts.

Serves 4–6

Liz Kuhlman

Shell's Shark

A piquant delight —

Grapefruit juice
1–2 jalapeño peppers, chopped (optional)
2 6- to 8-ounce Thresher shark steaks or
    swordfish steaks
Butter, melted

In a glass dish, combine the grapefruit juice and peppers and marinate the steaks for 30 minutes. Drain the steaks, brush all sides with melted butter, and grill over charcoal or mesquite wood for 3–4 minutes per side or until done.

Note: If desired, the steaks may be broiled rather than grilled.

Serves 2

Robert Hensleigh

Walnut-crusted Sole

A unique presentation of a welcome favorite —

4 fresh fillets of sole or flounder,* cut into
    serving-sized pieces
⅓ cup flour
Salt and pepper to taste
2 egg whites
3 tablespoons fine cracker crumbs
¾ cup walnuts, minced
4 tablespoons butter, clarified
1 tablespoon oil
1 lemon, quartered

Rinse the fillets, pat dry, and dredge in the combined flour, salt, and pepper. Beat the egg whites lightly. Dip the floured fillets in the egg whites and then in the combined cracker crumbs and walnuts, coating thoroughly each time, and set the fillets aside on a rack. Heat the butter and oil in a large skillet and sauté the fish over medium heat for about 3 minutes on each side, or until golden.

Garnish with the lemon wedges and serve.

This recipe is excellent for fresh fish but is not recommended for frozen fillets.

Serves 4

Arden Poole

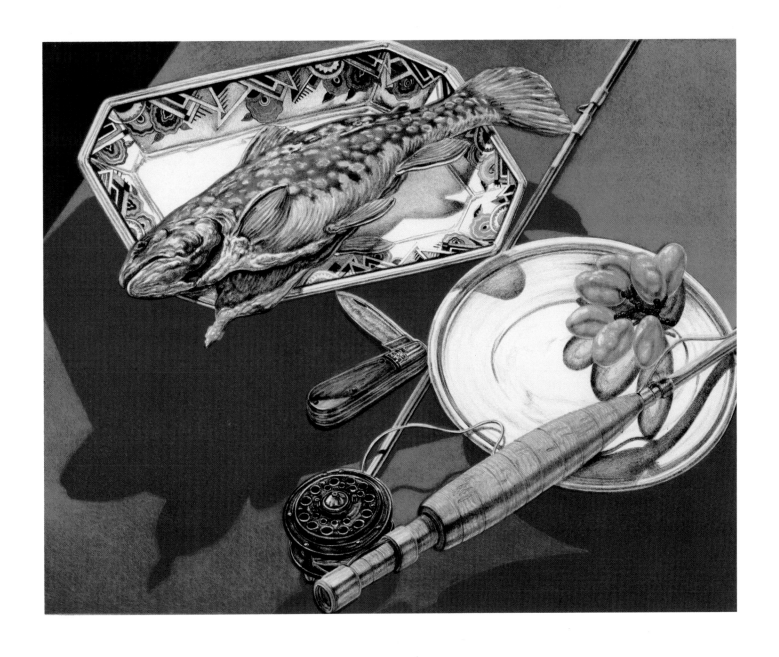

Jack Beal, American, b. 1931, *Trout*, 1977, lithograph, image: 50.8 x 66 cm; sheet: 63.5 x 77.5 cm. Founders Society Purchase, John S. Newberry Fund (F78.8).

Peruvian (Chimu), *Fish Effigy Vessel*, ca. 1200–1470, ceramic, h. 12.7 cm. Gift of Mr. and Mrs. Alger B. Scott (70.865).

Fillet de Poisson en Soufflé

A soupçon of Gruyère distinguishes this tempting fish soufflé.

½ pound fillet of sole or flounder
½ cup dry vermouth
¾ cup water (approximately)
¾ cup dry white wine
1 tablespoon shallots or green onions, minced
Salt and pepper to taste
2½ tablespoons butter
3 tablespoons flour
¾ cup milk, heated but not scalded
1 egg yolk
Dash of nutmeg
½ cup Gruyère cheese, grated coarsely
5 egg whites, beaten to stiff peaks
Sauce Mousseline Sabayon
     (recipe follows)

Place the fish in one layer in a shallow pan and add enough vermouth, water, and wine to cover. Add the shallots and seasonings and simmer uncovered about 6 minutes. Using a slotted spatula, remove the fish to a platter and keep warm. Over high heat, bring the remaining liquid to a boil, cook until reduced to ½ cup, and set aside.

Melt the butter in a saucepan, add the flour, and whisk to blend. Cook for 2 minutes (but do not let the flour brown) and remove the pan from the heat. Whisk in the hot milk and ¼ cup of the reserved cooking liquid (reserve the remaining ¼ cup for the sauce), bring to a boil, and stir for 1 minute. Remove the mixture from the heat, whisk in the egg yolk, salt and pepper to taste, and a dash of nutmeg. Stir in all but 2 tablespoons of the cheese.* Gently fold in one-quarter of the beaten egg whites and then the remaining whites, blending thoroughly.

Preheat the oven to 425°F. Lightly butter a shallow, oval, ovenproof casserole and spread a small amount of the soufflé mixture over the bottom to the depth of ¼-inch. Flake the poached fish and spread in an even layer over the soufflé mixture; top with the remaining soufflé mixture and sprinkle with the remaining cheese. Bake the soufflé for 15–18 minutes or until puffed and brown and serve with *Sauce Mousseline Sabayon*.

The soufflé mixture may be made ahead to this point.

Serves 4 as an entrée (or 6 as a first course)

Sauce Mousseline Sabayon

¾ cup butter
¼ cup liquid from poached fish
3 tablespoons heavy cream
4 egg yolks
Salt and white pepper to taste
1 teaspoon lemon juice (or to taste)

Divide the butter into six pieces and set aside. In the top of a double boiler, combine the reserved liquid from the poached fish, the cream, egg yolks, salt, pepper, and lemon juice. Place the pan over hot water (do not let the water touch the bottom of the pan and do not let the water boil) and using a whisk, blend one piece of the butter at a time into the sauce until it is thick and creamy. Taste and correct the seasonings and serve on the side with *Fillet de Poisson en Soufflé*.

Yields 1½ cups

Frederick J. Cummings

Shrimp Gumbo

Louisiana's pride and joy —

1/4 cup butter, melted
2 tablespoons flour
2 cloves garlic, minced
2 onions, chopped coarsely
1 green pepper, chopped coarsely
1 1-pound can tomatoes
1 pound fresh okra (or 2 10-ounce packages
    frozen okra)
1 6-ounce can tomato paste
2 beef bouillon cubes
1–2 tablespoons Worcestershire sauce
1/2 teaspoon chili powder
1/2 teaspoon cayenne pepper
1/2 teaspoon basil
1 bay leaf
1 1/2 tablespoons salt
1/4 teaspoon pepper
3 cups water
1 1/2 pounds raw shrimp, shelled and
    deveined
3 cups hot, cooked rice

In a Dutch oven over low heat, melt the
butter, stir in the flour, and cook until
the flour is lightly browned. Add the
garlic, onions, and green pepper and
cook until tender. Add the tomatoes and
the remaining ingredients, except for the
shrimp and the rice. Simmer the mixture, uncovered, for 45 minutes. Add the
shrimp, cover, and simmer for about 5
minutes or just until the shrimp is done
(do not overcook). Serve the gumbo in
shallow bowls over hot rice.

Note: The tomato sauce for the
gumbo may be prepared in advance and
frozen for later use.

Serves 8–10

Robert D. Nulf

Guo Xu, Chinese, 1456–after 1526, *Fisherman and Poem* (detail), Ming Dynasty, handscroll, ink on paper, 21.6 x 151.1 cm. Founders Society Purchase, Sarah Bacon Hill Fund (42.51).

Shrimp Turkolimano

A wonderful Mediterranean dish, discovered on a cruise ship in the Aegean —

1 tablespoon salt
2 cups milk
1 pound shrimp, shelled and deveined
Butter
1/4 cup white wine
1/4 cup Escargot Butter, melted
    (recipe follows)
1/2 teaspoon oregano
1/2 teaspoon pepper
2 large, ripe tomatoes, peeled, seeded, and
    chopped
1/4 pound feta cheese
Parmesan cheese, grated

Combine the salt and the milk, add the
shrimp, and soak for about 40 minutes.
Drain the shrimp, rinse in cold water,
and pat dry. Butter a shallow, ovenproof
pan, add the shrimp, white wine, and
Escargot Butter, season with oregano and
pepper, and stir in the chopped tomatoes. Crumble the feta cheese over the
top and sprinkle with the Parmesan
cheese. Bring the liquid to a boil over
medium heat and then place the pan under the broiler until the cheese melts.

Serves 4

Escargot Butter

1/2 cup unsalted butter
2 large shallots, minced
2 cloves garlic, minced
2 tablespoons fresh parsley, chopped

In a saucepan, melt the butter and add
the shallots, garlic, and parsley. Stir to
blend the ingredients thoroughly.

Yields 1/2 cup

Margie Gillis

Edward Steichen, American, 1879–1973, *Silverware Still Life,* 1930, gelatin-silver print, 20.6 x 16.5 cm. Founders Society Purchase, Henry E. and Consuelo S. Wenger Foundation Fund (F77.89).

Mussels Provençale

Classic French seasonings are the secret of this savory seafood mélange.

4 dozen mussels, scrubbed
2 cups red wine
2 cups tomato purée
1 medium onion, minced
4 cloves garlic, minced
2 tablespoons basil
1 tablespoon lemon juice
1 teaspoon salt
1 teaspoon black pepper
3 sprigs parsley, whole, and 4 tablespoons
    parsley, minced

4 tablespoons butter
Parmesan cheese, grated

Place all of the ingredients except for the minced parsley, butter, and Parmesan cheese, into a large kettle. Bring to a boil, cover, reduce the heat, and simmer for 10 minutes, stirring occasionally, or until the mussels have opened (discard any that are still closed). Place the mussels in individual soup bowls and set aside.

Add the butter to the kettle and cook over high heat until the liquid is reduced by one-half. Strain the broth, pour over the mussels, and sprinkle with the minced parsley and the Parmesan cheese.

Note: This delicious dish may also be served over pasta.

Serves 4–6

Nettie Firestone

Oriental Shrimp

A light and delectable Far Eastern treat —

2 tablespoons catsup
1 tablespoon oil
2 tablespoons Worcestershire sauce
2 teaspoons dry sherry or cognac
1 teaspoon sugar
6 drops hot pepper sauce
12 ounces fresh or frozen shrimp, shelled
    and deveined
2 teaspoons cornstarch combined with
    1 tablespoon cold water
2–3 cups hot, cooked rice

In a 1½-quart casserole, combine the catsup, oil, Worcestershire sauce, sherry, sugar, and hot pepper sauce. Add the shrimp, stir to coat, cover, and cook over high heat for 5 minutes or until the shrimp is no longer transparent. Remove the shrimp from the casserole, set aside, and keep warm.

Measure the remaining juices and, if necessary, add water to make ¾ cup of liquid and return to the casserole. Stir in

the cornstarch and cook over high heat 1–1½ minutes or until the mixture has thickened. Return the shrimp to the sauce, heat through, and serve over a bed of hot, cooked rice.

Serves 2–4

Anna Van Hull

Stir-fried Kentucky Wonders

Scrumptious scallops with a Southern accent!

2 tablespoons safflower oil
2 tomatoes, chopped coarsely
2 cloves garlic, crushed and minced finely
1 onion, chopped coarsely
1 pound fresh mushrooms, rinsed, drained,
    and halved
1 pound fresh green beans, cut into julienne
    strips

1 pound scallops, rinsed and drained
1 teaspoon sea salt

Heat a wok or heavy iron skillet, add the oil, and heat until hot but not smoking. Add the tomatoes, garlic, and onion and stir fry until soft. Add the mushrooms and green beans and stir fry until the beans turn bright green. Add the scal-

lops, season with sea salt, heat through, and serve immediately.

Note: As a variation, shrimp or crabmeat may be substituted for the scallops.

Serves 4

Gerry Stockfleth

POULTRY AND GAME

*P*oultry and a variety of game birds have long been a mainstay of the dining table. This is due not only to the relative ease of their preparation for consumption but also to their nutritional value, economy, and excellent flavor.

Besides their popularity in meals, birds are found in the art and mythology of all countries. Myths including Harpies, or monsters with the head and upper torso of a woman with the wings, tail, and talons of a bird, are prevalent in ancient Greek and Persian literature. Reflecting such fantastic myths is this late sixteenth- or early seventeenth-century Persian *Underglaze Painted Polychrome Plate,* upon which is depicted an unusual Harpy, with the body of a bird and the turbaned head of a Persian youth, standing at the edge of a pool and surrounded by blossoms.

Birds also figure prominently in scenes of nature by Asian artists. An exquisite example is *Reeds and Geese,* one of a pair of six-fold screens by seventeenth-century artist Kanō Tsunenobu, in which geese rest amid marsh reeds, rose mallow, and chrysanthemums or are airborne in a sky of gold.

Persian (Tabriz region), *Underglaze Painted Polychrome Plate,* Safavid Dynasty, late 16th-early 17th cent., glazed earthenware ("Kubachi" ware), diam. 33.8 cm. Matilda R. Wilson Fund (79.7).

Chicken Cynthia à la Champagne

From a small restaurant in San Francisco, a dish as pleasing to the eye as to the palate —

1 tablespoon oil
2 tablespoons butter
4 whole chicken breasts, skinned and boned
Salt to taste
¾ cup dry champagne (California Pinot
     Chardonnay may be substituted)
1 cup chicken broth
1 cup mushrooms, sliced
1 orange, peeled and cut into segments
½–1 cup seedless grapes

In a skillet, heat the oil and 1 tablespoon of the butter, add the chicken, salt to taste, and sauté until golden brown. Drain off the fat, add the champagne and chicken broth, and simmer uncovered for 20 minutes or until tender.

In a separate pan, sauté the mushrooms in the remaining butter, add the orange segments and the grapes, heat through (approximately 2–3 minutes), and pour over the chicken. Serve immediately.

Serves 4

Ruth Holcomb

François Marie Aloncle, French, active 1758-81, *Wine Glass Cooler (Verrière)*, 1767, soft-paste porcelain, 12.7 x 29.2 x 19.7 cm. Bequest of Mrs. Horace E. Dodge in memory of her husband (71.230).

Deviled Chicken

The prized recipe of a chef to the Royal Family of England, who graciously consented to share his secret —

4 large chicken breasts, skinned and boned
½ pint whipping cream
2 tablespoons Worcestershire sauce
2 tablespoons mushroom catsup*
1 tablespoon dry mustard
3 tablespoons mango chutney, puréed

Broil the chicken breasts 6 inches from the heat for 6 minutes on each side. While the chicken is broiling, whip the cream until stiff peaks form and fold in the remaining ingredients. Spoon the sauce over the chicken and place in a 400°F. oven for 10 minutes. Serve immediately.

This ingredient may be found in most specialty food stores.

Serves 4

Mrs. Walter B. Ford II

Chicken Saltimbocca

A zesty Italian delight —

3 large, whole chicken breasts, skinned,
     boned, and halved
12 thin slices prosciutto
6 thin slices mozzarella cheese
1 medium tomato, seeded and chopped
½ teaspoon sage or oregano
½ cup dry bread crumbs
2 tablespoons Parmesan cheese
2 tablespoons parsley, chopped
4 tablespoons butter, melted

Pound the chicken breasts until thin. Place 2 slices of the prosciutto and one slice of the mozzarella on each breast and sprinkle with some of the chopped tomato and sage or oregano. Carefully tuck in the sides of the fillets, roll up, and secure each with a toothpick.

In a small bowl, combine the bread crumbs, Parmesan, and parsley. Dip the chicken in the melted butter, roll in the crumb mixture, place in a shallow pan, and bake for 45 minutes or until chicken is tender.

Serves 4

Mollie Fletcher-Darr

Chicken Taos

Chili sauce and sherry combine to make this dish unique.

¼ cup flour
2 teaspoons seasoned salt
½ teaspoon pepper
12 pieces chicken
¼ cup butter
1 cup onion, chopped
½ teaspoon garlic powder
2 tablespoons Worcestershire sauce
1 cup chili sauce

1½ cups chicken stock
½ cup dry sherry
3 cups hot, cooked rice

Combine the flour, salt, and pepper and coat the chicken pieces thoroughly. In a large skillet, melt the butter and brown the chicken evenly on all sides. Add the onions, sauté until transparent, then add all of the remaining ingredients except for the rice. Bring to a boil, reduce the heat, and simmer covered for 35 minutes or until the chicken is tender. Serve the chicken and sauce over hot, cooked rice.
    Serves 6

Cynthia Jo Fogliatti

Peking Chicken with Peanuts

Oriental spice from the province of Hopei —

2–2½ pounds chicken breasts, skinned, boned, and cut into ½-inch pieces
1 egg white, beaten lightly
2 tablespoons cornstarch
1 teaspoon sugar
1 teaspoon salt
3 tablespoons vegetable oil
4 slices fresh ginger, shredded
4 cloves garlic, minced
½–1 teaspoon hot red pepper flakes
2 tablespoons soy sauce
2 tablespoons hoisin sauce
¼ cup chicken broth

4–6 scallions (with tops), cut into ½-inch pieces
1 cup peanuts or cashews

Marinate the chicken in a combination of the egg white, cornstarch, sugar, and salt for at least 30 minutes and drain. Heat the oil in a wok until hot but not smoking. Stir fry the chicken for 1 minute or until the meat turns white, and remove to a warm platter.
    Add the ginger, garlic, and red pepper flakes to the wok and stir fry for 15 seconds, then stir in the soy and hoisin sauces and the chicken broth. Return the chicken to the wok and cook just until heated through. Add the scallions and the nuts and serve immediately.
    Serves 8

Mrs. Michael Kan

Stuffed Chicken Breasts

Delicious served hot or cold, whole or sliced —

1 pound ricotta cheese
1 pound fresh spinach, chopped finely
3 small broccoli flowerets, chopped finely
Salt and pepper to taste
1 teaspoon thyme
1 teaspoon tarragon
4 whole chicken breasts, boned but not skinned
4 tablespoons butter

Preheat the oven to 350°F. In a large bowl, mix together the ricotta, spinach, broccoli, salt, pepper, thyme, and tarragon. Gently lift the skin from the chicken breasts to form a pocket and stuff with the cheese and spinach mixture. Tuck the sides of the breasts underneath, place in a shallow baking pan, and top each with 1 tablespoon of butter. Bake approximately 1 hour or until golden brown.
    Serves 4

Hadley Mack

Tarragon Rabbit

Succulent morsels simmered in a robust wine sauce —

2 rabbits, cleaned and cut into serving-
    sized pieces
¼ cup plus 2 tablespoons flour
¼ cup butter or margarine
4 tablespoons vegetable oil
1 large onion, diced
4 carrots, diced
3 cups veal or beef stock
1 cup dry white wine
2 tablespoons tarragon, crushed
1 teaspoon thyme
1 bay leaf
¾ cup sour cream
4 teaspoons Dijon mustard
Hot, buttered noodles

Sprinkle the rabbits lightly with ¼ cup of flour. In a large skillet, heat the butter or margarine and the vegetable oil, add the rabbit a few pieces at a time, and brown thoroughly. Remove and drain on paper towels.

Add the onion and carrots to the pan and sauté until the onion is translucent but not brown. Spoon off any grease and return the rabbit pieces to the skillet. Add the stock, wine, tarragon, thyme, and bay leaf, cover, and simmer over medium heat for 45 minutes or until the rabbit is tender.

In a small bowl, combine the sour cream, remaining 2 tablespoons of flour, and mustard and mix thoroughly. Stir in a small amount of the pan gravy, then return the sour cream and gravy mixture to the skillet and stir until thoroughly blended. Serve with hot, buttered noodles.

    Serves 6-8

Arden Poole

Jean B. C. Odiot, French, 1763–1850,
Wine Cooler (one of a pair), 1804, silver gilt,
h. 36.8 cm. Gift of Mrs. Roger Kyes in
memory of her husband (71.296).

Wild Duck Hash

A good way to use wild duck of doubtful age —

3 wild ducks, cleaned
3 strips bacon
¼ cup parsley
2 stalks celery, chopped
2 onions, 1 sliced and 1 chopped
½ green pepper, chopped
½ cup mushrooms, chopped
2 tablespoons butter
2 sprigs fresh thyme (or ½ teaspoon dried
    thyme)
2 tablespoons fresh dill weed, chopped (or ½
    teaspoon dried dill weed)
Salt and pepper to taste

Preheat the oven to 375°F. Place the ducks in a roasting pan with a strip of bacon over each duck's breast. Bake for 1½ hours, basting frequently, or until the ducks are tender. Cool completely, remove the meat from the bones, dice, and set aside.

In a saucepan, cover the duck carcasses with water, add the parsley, celery, and sliced onion, bring to a boil, and cook until the liquid is reduced to approximately 1½ cups; strain and set aside.

In a separate pan, sauté the chopped onion, green pepper, and mushrooms in the butter. Combine the sautéed vegetables, herbs, and the diced meat in a shallow casserole. Cover with the reduced broth, season with salt and pepper, and bake for 1 hour.

    Serves 8-10

Jean W. Hudson

Teriyaki Chicken Wings

A tantalizing Japanese-style entrée or hors d'oeuvres —

1/3 cup fresh lemon juice
1/4 cup soy sauce
1/4 cup vegetable oil
3 tablespoons chili sauce
2 cloves garlic, minced
1/4 teaspoon pepper
1/4 teaspoon celery seed
Dash of mustard
3 pounds chicken wings
Hot, cooked rice

Combine all of the ingredients except for the chicken and stir to blend. Cut the chicken wings at the joints, remove the wing tips, and place wings in a shallow baking dish. Add the marinade, cover, and refrigerate for at least 4 hours.

Drain and save the marinade to use as basting liquid. Place the wings on a broiler pan approximately 7 inches from the flame and broil 10 minutes on each side, brushing occasionally with the marinade. Serve with hot, cooked rice as a main dish or the wings alone as an appetizer.

Yields approximately 40

Annette Balian

Chicken with Grapes and Almonds

A favorite for formal dining —

6 chicken breasts
1/2 cup flour
1 teaspoon paprika
3/4 teaspoon salt
1/2 teaspoon pepper
2 tablespoons shallots or green onions, chopped
2 tablespoons butter
2 tablespoons oil
1/2 cup mushrooms, sliced

1/4 cup brandy
1/4 cup dry vermouth
1/2 cup chicken stock
1/2 cup seedless grapes
1/2 cup slivered almonds

Lightly coat the chicken breasts with the combined flour, paprika, salt, and pepper. In a large skillet, sauté the shallots in the butter and oil for 3 minutes, add the chicken, and brown lightly. Stir in the mushrooms. Add the brandy, ignite, and, when the flames die, add the vermouth and chicken stock. Cover and simmer for 15 minutes or until the chicken is tender. Add the grapes and almonds, heat through, and serve immediately.

Serves 6

Andrew L. Camden

Chicken Ratatouille

A mouthwatering Mediterranean mélange —

1/4 cup corn oil
2 whole chicken breasts, skinned, boned, and cut into 1-inch pieces
2 small zucchini, left unpeeled and sliced thinly
1 small eggplant, peeled and cut into 1-inch cubes
1 large onion, sliced thinly
1 medium green pepper, seeded and cut into 1-inch pieces
1/2 pound mushrooms, sliced

1 16-ounce can tomatoes, drained and cut into wedges
2 teaspoons garlic salt
1 teaspoon sweet basil
1 teaspoon dried parsley
1/2 teaspoon black pepper

Heat the oil in a large skillet and sauté the chicken breasts for approximately 2 minutes on each side. Add the zucchini, eggplant, onion, green pepper, and mushrooms and cook, stirring occasionally, for 15 minutes or until the vegetables are barely tender. Add the tomatoes and the seasonings and let simmer for 5 minutes or until the chicken is cooked through.

Serves 4

Mrs. Harvey C. Fruehauf, Jr.

Cuban Chicken

A scintillating combination with a Latin accent —

1 frying chicken, cut into serving-sized
    pieces (or 4 chicken breasts)
2 tablespoons or more oil
2 cloves garlic, pressed
1 large onion, chopped
1 large green pepper, chopped
4 small, thin-skinned potatoes, cubed
1/2 cup raisins
1/2 cup pitted, ripe olives
3/4 teaspoon oregano
3/4 teaspoon cumin

1 16-ounce can tomato sauce
1/3 cup dry white wine
1 cup frozen peas, thawed

In a Dutch oven, brown the chicken in the oil, remove to a platter, and drain all but 2 tablespoons of the oil from the pan. Add the garlic, onion, and green pepper to the pan and sauté until the onion is transparent.

Return the chicken to the pan and add all of the remaining ingredients except for the peas, bring to a boil, reduce the heat, cover, and cook for 30 minutes or until the chicken and the vegetables are tender. Stir in the peas, heat through, and serve.

Note: *Cuban Chicken* may be made in advance and reheated before serving.

Serves 3-4

Charlotte Rosenthal

Chicken with Lime Butter

The hint of lime is tangy and refreshing.

3 chicken breasts, skinned, boned, and
    halved
1/2 teaspoon salt
1/2 teaspoon pepper
1/3 cup vegetable oil
Juice of 1 large lime
8 tablespoons butter
1/2 teaspoon chives, minced
1/2 teaspoon dill weed

In a skillet over medium heat, season the chicken with salt and pepper and sauté in the oil for 4 minutes. Turn the chicken, cover the pan, reduce the heat, and cook for 10 minutes more. Remove the chicken and keep warm. Drain the oil from the pan, add the lime juice, and heat briefly. Add the butter and cook, stirring constantly, until the mixture be-gins to thicken. Stir in the chives and dill weed and serve the sauce over the chicken.

Serves 6

John Turner

Poulet à l'orange

A sunny flavor to evoke the French countryside —

4 tablespoons butter
1 frying chicken, cut into serving-sized
    pieces
3/4 teaspoon salt
1/8 teaspoon cayenne pepper
1 cup orange juice
1 tablespoon cornstarch
2 tablespoons cold water
2 tablespoons orange liqueur
1/4 teaspoon ground cloves
1 1/2 teaspoons orange rind, grated
1 clove garlic, pressed

1 1/2 cups orange sections
1 cup avocado, cut into cubes

In a large frying pan, melt the butter over medium heat and brown the chicken. Season the chicken with the salt and cayenne pepper, add the orange juice, cover, and simmer for 30 minutes or until tender. Remove the chicken from the pan and keep warm.

In a bowl, blend the cornstarch, cold water, and orange liqueur, add to the pan, and bring to a boil. Reduce the heat, add the cloves, orange rind, and garlic, and cook until the sauce thickens, stirring constantly. Remove the sauce from the heat and stir in the orange sections and the avocado cubes. Return the chicken to the pan, place over low heat, baste with the sauce until heated through, and serve.

Serves 4

Charlotte Rosenthal

Kanō Tsunenobu, Japanese, 1636–1713, *Reeds and Geese* (one of a pair of six-fold screens), 17th cent., ink, colors, and gold on paper, each screen 185.4 x 405.1 cm. Founders Society Purchase, Acquisitions Fund (80.43).

Canada Goose Stew

An entrée for cold days — delightful with wild rice and walnuts, green salad, and a hearty red wine such as Zinfandel.

1 Canada goose
1 medium onion, chopped finely
8 carrots, quartered
10 stalks celery, quartered
Salt, pepper, and poultry seasoning to taste
Water
3 tablespoons cornstarch combined with
    1 cup cold water
4–6 turnips, peeled and quartered

Place the goose in a large pot, add the onion, carrots, celery, seasonings, and water to cover, and simmer about 3 hours or until the goose is tender and the meat falls away from the bone. Let cool for several hours, discard the hardened fat, and reserve the stock. Remove the meat and set aside. Discard the bones and the skin.

Bring the goose stock to a slow boil, gradually add the combined cornstarch and water, and simmer, stirring constantly, until thickened. Season to taste and set aside.

In a separate pan, add the turnips and water to cover, cook until tender, and drain. Add the turnips and reserved meat to the stock, bring to a simmer, heat through, correct the seasonings, and serve.

Serves 6

Charles A. Muer

Chicken Piccata

Lemons and capers combined create magical flavor.

4 chicken breasts, skinned, boned, and
    halved
½ cup flour
1½ teaspoons salt
¼ teaspoon freshly ground pepper
Paprika to taste
¼ cup butter
1 tablespoon olive oil
2–4 tablespoons water
3 tablespoons fresh lemon juice
1 large lemon, sliced thinly
3–4 tablespoons capers (optional)
¼ cup fresh parsley, minced

Place the chicken breasts between sheets of waxed paper and pound until they are about ¼-inch thick. Combine the flour, salt, pepper, and paprika in a bag, add the chicken breasts, and shake to coat well.

In a large skillet, heat the butter and oil until bubbling and sauté the chicken breasts, a few at a time, for 2-3 minutes per side (do not overcook). Drain the breasts on paper towels and keep warm.

Discard all but 3 tablespoons of the butter and oil from the pan, add the water, and stir to deglaze. Stir in the lemon juice, heat briefly, and return the chicken to the skillet. Add the lemon slices, cook until the sauce begins to thicken, add the capers, and sprinkle the chicken with minced parsley. Serve immediately.

Serves 6–8

Lois Stulberg

Marinated Chicken Livers

A crowd-pleasing adaptation of the Chinese delicacy —

2 tablespoons honey
2 tablespoons soy sauce
¼ cup corn oil
1 tablespoon white wine
1 clove garlic, crushed
1 pound chicken livers, rinsed, drained, and
    trimmed

Hot, cooked rice
1–2 green onions, chopped

Preheat the oven to 375°F. Combine the honey, soy sauce, corn oil, wine, and garlic and blend thoroughly. Add the chicken livers and marinate for 30 min-utes at room temperature. Place the livers and marinade in a greased, shallow baking dish and bake for 25 minutes. Serve over hot, cooked rice garnished with chopped green onions.

Serves 2–4

Elizabeth A. Ricker

Roast Partridge with Cold Orange Sauce

A superb treatment for all types of game —

3 partridges
Salt and pepper to taste
White grapes
3 tablespoons butter, melted
½ cup sherry
Cold Orange Sauce
    (recipe follows)

Preheat the oven to 375°F. Rinse the partridges quickly and pat dry inside and out. Season the cavities with salt and pepper and stuff with the grapes.

Place the partridges in a casserole and bake uncovered for 15 minutes, basting at least three times with the melted butter. Reduce the heat to 325°F., pour the sherry over the partridges, cover, and cook for 45 minutes or until tender. Serve with *Cold Orange Sauce*.

Serves 6

Cold Orange Sauce

6 tablespoons currant jelly
3 tablespoons sugar
Rind of 2 oranges, grated
2 tablespoons port
2 tablespoons lemon juice
2 tablespoons orange juice
¼ teaspoon salt

In a small bowl, combine the jelly, sugar, and orange rind and beat for 5 minutes. Add the remaining ingredients and stir until well blended. Refrigerate until needed.

Yields approximately 1 cup

Linda VanLokeren

Chutney-glazed Chicken Breasts

Influenced by East Indian cuisine —

4 tablespoons butter
4 whole chicken breasts, boned and halved
    but not skinned
1⅓ cups water
⅔ cup chutney, chopped*
2 teaspoons cornstarch, combined with a
    little cold water

Preheat the oven to 325°F. In a heavy skillet, melt the butter and brown the chicken on all sides. Place the chicken in a shallow roasting pan and set aside.

Add the water and chutney to the skillet, deglaze the pan, and pour over the chicken. Cover the roasting pan with heavy-duty foil and seal the edges well. Bake for 30 minutes, basting several times or until the chicken is tender, and remove to a warm platter.

Add the combined cornstarch and water to the pan juices, heat, and stir until thickened. Serve the chutney glaze over the chicken breasts.

*Rafetto Chutney is recommended as it is already chopped finely and has a rich flavor.

Serves 4–6

Lois Stulberg

Persian (Shiraz[?], south-central Iran), *Rosewater Sprinkler,* 18th–19th cent., glass, h. 36.5 x diam. 10.5 cm. Founders Society Purchase, H. C. Wenger Foundation Fund (76.72).

Roast Wild Duck Star O'Brien

A perfect entrée for autumn entertaining —

1 small duck per person (or 1 large duck
    for two)
Madeira Sauce or Game Sauce
    (recipes follow)

Preheat the oven to 450°F. Wash the
ducks, remove any pinfeathers, and place
in an open roasting pan. Roast for 25
minutes — the ducks will be rare — and
set aside to cool (reserve the pan juices).
    Remove the breasts and legs from
the carcass, discard the skin covering the
breasts, cover, and refrigerate. Before
serving, remove the ducks from the refrigerator and let stand until room
temperature.
    In a skillet, add the *Madeira Sauce*

or *Game Sauce* and the pieces of duck,
heat through, and serve immediately.
    Note: This dish must be prepared in
advance.

Madeira Sauce

3 tablespoons butter
3 tablespoons currant jelly
3 tablespoons Madeira
Juice from the roasted ducks, defatted

In a small saucepan, melt the butter and
the jelly, add the Madeira and the defatted juice from the ducks, and stir to
blend well.
    Yields 1 cup

Game Sauce

6 ounces currant jelly
½ teaspoon dry mustard
1 tablespoon frozen orange juice, undiluted
1 tablespoon lemon juice
¼ cup red wine

In a jar, combine all of the ingredients
and shake vigorously. Refrigerate until
needed.
    Yields 1 cup

Betsy Campbell

Chicken in Mushroom Sauterne Sauce

A recipe of classic simplicity —

Salt to taste
12 chicken breasts, boned
2 cups sour cream
6 tablespoons flour
2 10¾-ounce cans mushroom soup
1 cup sauterne
2 teaspoons paprika

4 ounces pimento, drained and sliced
1 cup sliced almonds

Preheat the oven to 325°F. Lightly salt
the chicken breasts and arrange in one
layer in 1 or 2 greased baking dishes.
Blend together the sour cream and flour,

combine with the soup and sauterne,
pour over the chicken, and sprinkle with
paprika. Arrange the pimento and the almonds over the top and bake for 1½
hours or until the chicken is tender.
    Serves 8–12

Doreen Millman

Chicken and Zucchini in Cream

The zucchini adds an unusual dimension to this rich dish.

6 tablespoons butter
4 small zucchini, cut into julienne strips
1 teaspoon marjoram
2 whole chicken breasts, skinned, boned,
    and cut into julienne strips
1 cup whipping cream
Salt and pepper to taste
Hot, cooked rice

In a wok or large skillet, melt 3 tablespoons of the butter, add the zucchini,
season with the marjoram, and stir fry
for approximately 3–4 minutes or just
until tender. Remove the zucchini from
the pan and set aside. Add the remaining
butter and the chicken, stir fry for 3–5
minutes, and remove from the pan. Add
the cream and cook, stirring constantly,

until the cream has thickened and has
been reduced by one-half. Return the
zucchini and the chicken to the pan, heat
through, salt and pepper to taste, and
serve over the cooked rice.
    Serves 4

Margie Gillis

Cold Boned Chicken

Though complex, this recipe is well worth the effort, especially to cool a hot summer evening.

1 3½-pound chicken, boned but not skinned
Salt and pepper to taste
¼ pound prosciutto or baked Virginia ham,
    sliced thinly
⅓ cup moist Duxelles
    (recipe follows)
¼ cup parsley
1 teaspoon tarragon
¼ cup pine nuts
10 pitted black olives, sliced
2 large eggs, hard-boiled
¼ cup fine bread crumbs
Unsalted butter, softened
2 strips bacon, halved
Dry white wine (optional)
Tomatoes, sliced (optional)
Watercress (optional)
Chicken aspic, diced (optional)
Mayonnaise Sauce
    (recipe follows)

Place the chicken skin side down on a piece of waxed paper, arrange in a rectangle, and sprinkle with salt and pepper. Cover with another sheet of waxed paper, pound gently with a mallet or rolling pin until of a uniform thickness, and remove the top piece of paper. Cover the chicken with the prosciutto and spread with the *Duxelles*, parsley, tarragon, pine nuts, and olives. Arrange the whole eggs lengthwise down the middle of the chicken and sprinkle again with salt and pepper.

Using the waxed paper as an aid, bring up the sides of the chicken skin and fasten together temporarily with skewers. Tie string or thread around the roll in two places and gently pull the skin so that it overlaps along the entire length of the roll. Tuck in the ends neatly and sew up the seams with strong thread. Remove the skewers, pat the roll into a uniform shape, and rub the entire outside with the unsalted butter. Arrange the strips of bacon across the top of the roll, place in a shallow baking pan, and bake for 50 minutes at 350°F. If the chicken begins to look dry, baste with a combination of melted butter and white wine. Remove the strips of bacon, raise the temperature to 425°F., and cook for 10 minutes more to brown the skin. Remove the roll from the oven, cool at room temperature, wrap in foil, and refrigerate for at least 8 hours.

Cut away the strings and thread and place the chicken in the freezer for 25–30 minutes. Remove the skin and slice the roll. Spoon a little of the *Mayonnaise Sauce* onto a platter, place the chicken slices in two rows down the center, and cover with additional sauce (remaining sauce may be served on the side). Garnish the platter with sliced tomatoes, additional black olives or parsley, watercress, or diced chicken aspic.

Note: Try this entrée accompanied by a curried rice salad (see recipes on pp. 40 and 46).
Serves 8

Duxelles

¼ pound mushrooms, minced
1½ tablespoons butter
1 tablespoon shallots or scallions, minced
¼ teaspoon pepper
¼ teaspoon tarragon
1 tablespoon flour
2 tablespoons port or Madeira
¼ cup heavy cream

Wrap the mushrooms in cheesecloth and squeeze all of the moisture from them. In a skillet, melt the butter, add the shallots and the mushrooms, and cook over high heat, stirring constantly, until the mushrooms separate. Add the seasonings, blend in the flour, and stir for 2 minutes. Stir in the port and the cream, bring to a boil, and cook until the mixture has thickened. Taste and correct seasonings.

Note: *Duxelles* may be prepared in advance and frozen for later use.
Yields 1 cup

Mayonnaise Sauce

¼ cup Homemade Mayonnaise
    (see recipe p. 122)
½ cup heavy cream, whipped
2 teaspoons chicken concentrate
1 tablespoon parsley, chopped

Combine all of the ingredients, mix thoroughly, and chill before using.
Yields ¾ cup

Bishie Beatty

Polynesian (Hawaiian Islands), *Calabash*, ca. 1800, calabash, h. 31.8 cm. Gift of Walter Randel (77.26).

Chicken in Pipian Sauce

Spoon up the sauce with hot tortillas!

*1 frying chicken, cut into serving-sized
    pieces*
1/2–3/4 cup cooking oil
Pipian Sauce (recipe follows)
1/2 cup peanuts
Salt to taste
Tortillas (optional)

In a skillet, sauté the chicken in the oil
until golden brown, drain, and remove
to a platter. Add the *Pipian Sauce* to the
skillet, heat, add the chicken, and cook
over low heat for 10–15 minutes or until
the chicken is tender and completely
coated with the sauce. Add the peanuts
and salt to taste. Heat the tortillas briefly
in the oven and serve on the side.
    Serves 4–6

Pipian Sauce*

6–8 chiles anchos
1 cup boiling water
1/2 cup dry corn, toasted

1 cup pumpkin or sunflower seeds, toasted
1/2 cup unsalted peanuts
2 cloves garlic
1 quart chicken broth
1/4 cup cooking oil
Salt to taste

Wash and dry the chiles, remove the
seeds, and soak in the boiling water for
30 minutes or more. In a blender or food
processor, combine the chiles and water
with the corn, pumpkin seeds, peanuts,
and garlic and process. Add one-half of
the chicken broth to the chile mixture
and put through a food mill or coarse
sieve.
    In a skillet, heat the oil, add the
chile mixture, and simmer until it begins
to thicken. Add the remaining broth and
stir to blend.
    *Pipian Sauce may also be purchased
in a Mexican grocery or specialty food store.*
    Yields approximately 4 cups

Joy Emery

Country-style Chicken

An American regional recipe at its best —

1/2 cup fine, dry bread crumbs
2 tablespoons Parmesan cheese, grated
1 teaspoon basil
1 teaspoon oregano
1/2 teaspoon garlic salt
1/4 teaspoon salt
2 whole chicken breasts, halved
2/3 cup butter, melted
1/4 cup dry white wine (or apple juice)
1/4 cup green onion, chopped
1/4 cup fresh parsley, chopped

Preheat the oven to 375°F. Combine the
bread crumbs, cheese, basil, oregano,

garlic salt, and salt. Dip the chicken
breasts in 1/3 cup melted butter, then in
the crumb mixture, and place in an ungreased 9-inch baking dish, skin side up.
Bake for 45 minutes to 1 hour or until
the chicken is tender and golden brown.
Add the wine, green onion, and parsley
to the remaining butter, pour over and
around the chicken, and bake for an additional 15 minutes. Serve immediately
with the sauce spooned over the chicken.
    Serves 4

Susan Kahn-Sovel

Indian (Tamil Nadu), *Pārvatī, Consort of
Śiva*, 13th cent., bronze, h. with pedestal
103.8 cm. Founders Society Purchase, Sarah
Bacon Hill Fund (41.81).

Lingonberry Roast Duck

A tantalizing variation on the traditional duck —

2 4½-pound ducks
1 clove garlic
½ lemon, halved
Salt and pepper to taste
½ teaspoon fennel seed
½ teaspoon rosemary
1 orange, halved
½ onion, halved
⅓ cup honey
½ cup plus 2 tablespoons port
½ cup cranberry juice
½ cup orange juice
Chicken stock (optional)
3 tablespoons currant jelly
½ cup lingonberries
2 tablespoons cornstarch
2 tablespoons orange-flavored liqueur,
    heated (optional)

Preheat the oven to 375°F. Wash the ducks, pat dry, and rub the skins with the garlic and lemon quarters (reserve the lemon quarters). Sprinkle the cavity of each duck with salt, pepper, fennel seed, and rosemary. Stuff the ducks with the lemon quarters, orange halves, and onion quarters, place on a rack in a shallow baking pan, and roast for 35 minutes. Turn the ducks occasionally, basting with the natural juices, so as to brown evenly on all sides.

Reduce the heat to 350°F., season the ducks with additional salt and pepper, and continue roasting, without basting further, for approximately 1 hour or until tender. Remove the ducks from the oven, halve lengthwise, discard the bones, and place the meat in a shallow, ungreased pan. Brush the duck meat with honey and return to the oven until the honey melts (about 5 minutes).

Turn off the heat but leave the ducks in the oven to keep warm. Pour off the drippings from the roasting pan and skim off the fat. In the same roasting pan combine ½ cup of the port, the cranberry juice, and the orange juice. Add the drippings and cook over medium heat for about 5 minutes, stirring to deglaze the pan.

Measure the liquid — there should be 3–4 cups — and add chicken stock if necessary. Add the currant jelly and ¼ cup of the lingonberries and stir until well blended. Dissolve the cornstarch in the remaining 2 tablespoons of port, stir into the pan juices, bring to a boil, stir again, and correct the seasonings. Place the ducks on a serving platter, cover with one-half of the sauce, and garnish with the remaining lingonberries.

The duck may be flamed at the table by pouring heated orange liqueur over the duck and igniting. Serve with the remaining sauce on the side.

Serves 6

Lee Henkin

Chicken and Dumplings

Hearty and satisfying family fare —

1 stewing hen, disjointed
1½ quarts water
Salt and pepper to taste
1 onion
3 stalks celery
1 carrot
Dash of rosemary
6½ tablespoons flour combined with ¾ cup
    water
⅔ cup milk
1 egg
1 tablespoon cooking oil
1½ cups flour
⅔ teaspoon salt
4 teaspoons baking powder

In a large pot, combine the chicken, water, and salt and pepper to taste, then add the onion, celery, carrot, and rosemary. Cook over medium heat for 2 hours or until the chicken is tender. Remove the chicken from the broth (reserve the broth) and let cool. Remove the meat from the bones and dice. Strain the broth, thicken with the flour and water mixture, and stir until smooth. Remove 4 cups of the gravy to a shallow stewing pan and set aside. Return the chicken to the remaining gravy and keep warm.

In a large bowl, combine the milk, egg, and oil, sift in the flour, salt, and baking powder, and stir until well blended. In the stewing pan, bring the 4 cups of gravy to a boil. Drop large teaspoonsful of the dumpling batter into the boiling gravy, cover, and simmer gently for 10 minutes or until the dumplings are done. Serve with the chicken and gravy.

Serves 4

Esther G. Edwards

MEAT

*O*ften seen as an essential form of sustenance, meats have played a central role in mankind's existence. This is reflected not only in cave paintings, in which the capture of animals for food and hides is a recurrent theme, but also in Egyptian art, seventeenth-century Dutch and Flemish still lifes, and eighteenth-century French art. The variety of game and other foods depicted in such carvings or paintings was usually intended as a testament to the prosperity of the patron who had commissioned the work.

The subject of this painting is the call to dinner at the end of the workday. Let *The Dinner Horn,* by Winslow Homer, summon you to the wealth of dishes that are offered here for your dining pleasure. Whether served from a lovely porcelain dish such as the *Platter* from the *Swan Service,* modeled by Johann Joachim Kändler in 1737/41, from silver platters chased with lavish decoration, or "family style" from earthenware plates, these recipes lend themselves equally to great occasions or everyday meals.

Winslow Homer, American, 1836–1910, *The Dinner Horn* (detail), 1875, oil on canvas, 30.2 x 36.2 cm. Gift of Dexter M. Ferry, Jr. (47.81).

Jerry Crowley's 'Steak in a Paper Bag'

The cut of the meat is the secret to this recipe's success.

4 tablespoons butter, softened
4 tablespoons vegetable oil
1–2 cloves garlic, crushed
2 teaspoons seasoned salt
Pepper to taste
1 cup sharp Cheddar cheese, grated
1 cup egg bread crumbs
1 2½- to 3-pound boneless top sirloin steak
    (2½–3 inches thick, trimmed)

Mix together the butter, oil, garlic, salt, and pepper and set aside. Combine the cheese and the bread crumbs and set aside. Cover the steak on both sides with the butter mixture and then coat with the cheese and crumb mixture, covering thoroughly. Place the steak on a flattened brown paper bag just large enough to fit, slip it into a larger brown paper bag, fold over the end, and staple shut.

Place the bag on a baking sheet in a 375°F. oven and bake for 30 minutes for rare (an additional 10 minutes or so for medium). When done, remove the meat from the bag, return to the baking sheet, and place under the broiler about 3–4 inches from the flame. Broil for 2–3 minutes to brown the crumbs lightly. Slice the steak thinly and serve.

Serves 6

The Cookbook Committee

Spicy Lamb

A Middle Eastern experience —

1 pound lamb, ground
1 egg
1 small onion, chopped
2 tablespoons fresh parsley, chopped
1 clove garlic, chopped
¼ teaspoon each ginger, coriander,
    turmeric, and red pepper
Salt to taste

Plain yogurt
Rice, cooked

Combine the lamb with the rest of the ingredients, except for the yogurt and rice. Divide the mixture into four portions and form into patties. In a frying pan, sauté the patties until cooked through, remove from the pan, and keep warm. Add a little yogurt to the pan, stir until thoroughly heated, and pour over the patties. Serve the lamb and sauce with the hot, cooked rice.

Serves 4

Eve Cockburn

Company Casserole

The solution when entertaining large groups —

7 ounces noodles
3 tablespoons butter, melted
½ cup scallions or onions, chopped coarsely
¼ cup green pepper, chopped coarsely
1 tablespoon pimento, drained
2 tablespoons chives, chopped coarsely
1 cup cottage cheese
⅓ cup sour cream
6 ounces cream cheese
Salt and pepper to taste
2–3 pounds lean ground beef
2 8-ounce cans tomato sauce
Worcestershire sauce to taste
Tabasco sauce to taste

Cook the noodles, drain, and toss with the melted butter. In a food processor, dice (but do not purée) the scallions, green pepper, pimento, and chives. Add the cottage cheese, sour cream, cream cheese, salt, and pepper, process briefly to blend, and set aside.

In a skillet, brown the beef, drain off the fat, and stir in the tomato, Worcestershire, and Tabasco sauces. Cover the bottom of an open casserole with a thin layer of the meat sauce. Top the sauce with one-half of the noodles and all of the cheese mixture. Add layers of the remaining noodles and meat sauce,* bake at 350°F. for 50–60 minutes, and serve.

*The casserole may be made in advance up to this point and refrigerated.

Serves 6–8

Ann and Willis Woods

Steak and Kidney Pie

An English classic, as traditional as its country of origin —

3 lamb kidneys
1 cup plus 2 tablespoons flour, sifted
1 teaspoon salt
⅓ cup shortening
3–4 tablespoons cold water
1 large onion, chopped
4 tablespoons butter
1½ pounds round steak or sirloin tip, trimmed and cut into bite-sized pieces
1⅓ cups boiling water
1 tablespoon Worcestershire sauce
¼ teaspoon black pepper

Split the kidneys, remove the fat and the tubes, and soak in cold, salted water for 30 minutes. In a small bowl, combine 1 cup of the flour, ½ teaspoon of the salt, and cut in the shortening with a pastry blender or fork until the mixture resembles coarse meal. Stir in 3–4 tablespoons cold water, shape the dough into a ball, divide into two portions, and roll out each on a floured board — one-half to fit the bottom of a shallow, ovenproof casserole and one-half as the top crust — and set aside.

Sauté the onion in 2 tablespoons of the butter, add the steak or sirloin tip, and brown well. Add the boiling water, the Worcestershire sauce, and the pepper, cover, and simmer for 1 hour or until the meat is tender. Finely chop the kidneys, sauté in the remaining 2 tablespoons of butter for 10 minutes, and add to the steak. Thicken the gravy by mixing the remaining 2 tablespoons of flour with a little cold water and stirring to blend thoroughly. Transfer the mixture to the casserole, cover with the top crust, and trim with pastry scrolls, piercing in a large X to vent the heat. Bake the pie for 20–30 minutes at 400°F.

Serves 4–6

John C. Emery

Alfie's Hot Chile Mole

Spicy cuisine from South of the Border —

½ cup peanut or corn oil
2 pounds round beef steak, cut into ¾-inch cubes
1 pound lean, boneless pork or veal, cut into 1-inch cubes
1½ pounds Italian sausage (with fennel), cut into ½-inch slices
4 tablespoons cumin
1 pound slab bacon, cut into 1-inch cubes
3 large red onions, chopped coarsely
2 medium white onions, diced
6 small, hot green peppers, seeded and diced
6 jalapeño peppers, seeded and diced (or 1 4-ounce can green chilies, chopped)
2 large green bell peppers, seeded and diced
1 large red bell pepper, seeded and diced
2 large cloves garlic, chopped
1 large bunch celery, diced
1 12-ounce bottle beer
5 bay leaves
3 tablespoons chili powder
1 tablespoon celery salt
1 tablespoon freshly ground black pepper
1½ teaspoons allspice
1 tablespoon basil
1 teaspoon oregano
1 tablespoon dried dill (or one small bunch of fresh dill, chopped)
3 1-pound cans whole tomatoes (with liquid), chopped
2¾ cups tomato juice
2 6-ounce cans tomato purée
6 ounces unsweetened chocolate

Heat ¼ cup of the oil in a large frying pan, add the beef, pork, and sausage, sprinkle with 2 tablespoons of the cumin, and sauté until the meat is no longer pink. Drain off the fat and place in a large soup pot.

Fry the bacon until almost crisp, drain, and add to the meat in the pot. Add the remaining oil to the pan and sauté the onions, all of the peppers, garlic, and celery, and cook until the onions become transparent; transfer the vegetables to the soup pot. Add beer to cover the meat and vegetables and simmer uncovered for 30 minutes. Add the spices, chopped tomatoes, tomato juice, and tomato purée, and simmer uncovered for another 2 hours. Remove the bay leaves.

Melt the chocolate in a double boiler and stir into the soup pot. Cook and stir approximately 10 minutes more or until the chocolate is well blended and the mixture is heated through. Serve the chili in large bowls with crackers, warm tortillas, or French bread.

Serves 15

A. Alfred Taubman

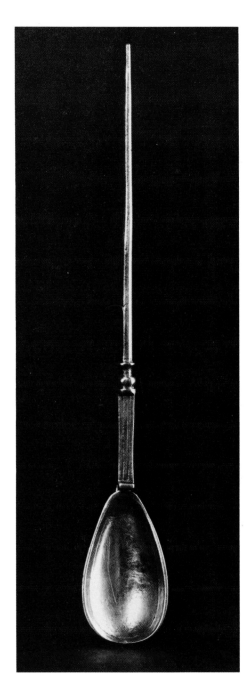

Roman, *Spoon,* 4th cent., silver, l. 16 cm.
Gift of Lillian Henkel Haass (50.86).

Oxtail Stew

As easy on the pocketbook as it is on the palate —

⅓ cup flour
2 teaspoons salt (or to taste)
Black pepper to taste
4 tablespoons butter
5 pounds oxtails (about 3)
1 cup plus 2 tablespoons Madeira
1 tomato, peeled and chopped
2 onions, chopped
2 cloves garlic, minced
1 large carrot, quartered, and 6 medium
    carrots, sliced
1 white turnip, quartered
Few sprigs parsley
1 bay leaf
2 10½-ounce cans beef consommé
1 cup water
6 leeks, sliced
Arrowroot or cornstarch (optional)

Combine the flour, salt, and pepper, and dredge the oxtails. In a heavy 4-quart casserole, melt the butter, brown the oxtails, remove the meat, and pour off the fat. Add 2 tablespoons of the Madeira and cook over low heat, stirring to deglaze the pan. Return the meat to the pan and add the tomato, onions, garlic, quartered carrot, turnip, parsley, bay leaf, consommé, and water. Bring to a boil, reduce the heat, cover tightly, and simmer for 3 hours.

Let the stew cool thoroughly, remove the meat, cover, and refrigerate overnight. Strain the broth and store uncovered one more night in the refrigerator. The next day, remove the fat from the broth, return the broth to the casserole, and let come to a boil over medium heat. Add the remaining cup of Madeira, taste, and correct the seasonings. Add the sliced carrots and leeks, return the meat to the pot, and let simmer until the vegetables are tender and the meat is heated through (about 25 minutes). For a thicker gravy, add a little arrowroot or cornstarch that has been mixed with cold water and stir to blend thoroughly.
    Serves 6

Margie Gillis

Veau aux Poires

Create a romantic aura with the delicate flavor combination of veal and pears.

12 ounces veal scaloppine
¼ cup flour
Salt and pepper to taste
4 tablespoons butter
2 pears, peeled, cored, and cut into six slices
    each
2 tablespoons brandy
1 cup heavy cream

Dredge the veal in the flour, season with the salt and pepper, and sauté in the butter for 1 minute on each side. Add the pears and cook until they are warmed through. Remove the veal and pears to a platter and keep warm.

Remove the pan from the heat, immediately add the brandy, and ignite. When the flames die, add the cream and cook over medium heat for 5 minutes. Pour the cream sauce over the veal and pears and serve immediately.
    Serves 2–4

Diane Schoenith

Pork Carbonnade with Caraway Noodles

Slowly simmered in beer and served over buttery noodles with caraway seeds —

¼ cup flour
Salt and pepper to taste
2 pounds boneless pork, cut into 1-inch
    pieces
3 tablespoons oil or butter
2–3 onions, sliced thinly
½ teaspoon thyme
1 12-ounce can light beer
1 small bay leaf
1 small bunch fresh parsley (or 2
    tablespoons dried parsley)
1½ cups carrots, cut into 2-inch pieces

½ pound broad noodles, cooked
2 tablespoons butter
1 teaspoon caraway seeds

Combine the flour, salt, and pepper and toss with the pork. In a large skillet, brown the pork in the oil or butter, add the onions, and sauté until the onions become glazed. Add the thyme and beer, tie the bay leaf and three of the parsley stems together, and add them to the skillet.* Cover and simmer until the meat is tender (about 1½ hours). Add the carrots and cook until tender.

Toss the cooked noodles with the 2 tablespoons butter and the caraway seeds. Serve the pork over the noodles and garnish with additional fresh chopped parsley.

*Remove the herb bundle before serving.

Serves 4–6

Cynthia Newman Helms

Liver with Apples and Onions

The garnish gives a matchless flavor to the meat.

4 slices calf's liver
1 cup milk
¼ cup flour
Salt and pepper to taste
4 tablespoons butter
1 medium onion, sliced
1 apple, cored and sliced

Soak the liver in milk for 1 hour, dry well, coat lightly with flour, and season to taste with salt and pepper. Melt 2 tablespoons of the butter in a pan and fry the liver over high heat, browning quickly on both sides; remove from the pan and keep warm.

Add the remaining butter to the pan, deglaze, and sauté the onion briefly. Add the apple slices, cover the pan, and cook over low heat for 5 minutes. Uncover the pan, raise the heat, and cook for 1–2 minutes more. Serve the liver topped with the onions and apples.

Serves 2

Kaia Lohmann

Veal Scaloppine with Mustard Sauce

A tangy variation on the classic recipe —

¾ pound veal scaloppine
⅓ cup flour
Salt and freshly ground pepper to taste
4 tablespoons butter
2 tablespoons shallots, minced
¼ cup dry white wine
½ cup heavy cream
1 tablespoon Dijon mustard
1 teaspoon mustard seeds
Fine egg noodles, cooked

Pound the scaloppine thin with the flat side of a meat mallet or the bottom of a skillet. Blend the flour with the salt and pepper and dredge the scaloppine thoroughly. Heat the butter in a large, heavy skillet until hot but not browned. Add the scaloppine and cook quickly until golden (about 2 minutes per side; note that they shrink as they cook). Remove the scaloppine to a warmed dish, cover with foil, and keep warm.

Add the shallots to the skillet and cook briefly. Add the wine and cook, stirring constantly, until it is almost evaporated. Stir in the cream and bring to a boil. Cook for 30 seconds, stirring constantly, turn off the heat, and blend in the mustard and mustard seeds. Spoon the sauce over the meat and serve with buttered noodles.

Serves 3–4

Mrs. Peter W. Stroh

Filet de Boeuf au Poivre

The bite of pepper highlights the tenderest of beef—

1 filet mignon or tournedo of beef
Olive oil
Black pepper, ground coarsely
2 dried mushrooms, soaked in warm water
　　for 15–20 minutes and drained
2 fresh mushrooms
1 tablespoon butter
Salt to taste
2 tablespoons brandy
1–2 tablespoons heavy cream
Parsley, chopped

Brush the filet with the olive oil, roll in the pepper (pressing the pepper into the meat), and set aside. Slice both the dried and fresh mushrooms and sauté in the butter until all of the liquid has been absorbed; set aside.

Heat a heavy skillet until a drop of water skitters across the surface of the pan. Sprinkle salt in the pan and sauté the meat until rare (about 2 minutes per side), remove, and keep warm. Add the brandy to the pan and, when warmed through, ignite. Let the flames die, add the mushrooms and cream, and, while stirring constantly, let come to a boil to thicken; correct seasonings to taste. Pour the sauce over the filets, sprinkle with a little chopped parsley, and serve immediately.

Serves 1

Patrice Marandel

Bigos

This traditional, hearty shepherd's stew will add warmth to a cold winter's night.

1 head cabbage
Salt
1 quart sauerkraut, rinsed thoroughly
1 slice bacon
½ pound pork, beef, or lamb, cooked and cut
　　into bite-sized pieces
1 pound Polish sausage, cooked and cut into
　　bite-sized pieces
1 large onion, chopped
¼ pound mushrooms, sliced
1 cup wine, water, or vegetable stock

Quarter the cabbage and boil or steam for 15 minutes or until tender. Thinly slice the cabbage, sprinkle with salt, and let stand for 1 hour. In a deep pot, cook the sauerkraut for 15–20 minutes or until tender. Press all moisture from the cabbage, add to the pot with the sauerkraut, and set aside.

In a large skillet, fry the bacon, add the chopped meats, onion, and mushrooms, and cook until the onion becomes translucent. Add the meat mixture and wine, water, or stock to the pot, simmer for about 45 minutes, and serve.

Note: The flavor of the stew improves with reheating.

Serves 12

Mrs. George Puscas

Glazed Corned Beef

The glaze adds a special quality—

1 whole corned beef (approximately
　　8 pounds)
Boiling water
1 12-ounce can beer
1 tablespoon mixed pickling spices
½ cup brown sugar, packed firmly
⅓ cup prepared mustard

Preheat the oven to 325°F. Quickly rinse the beef and place in a roasting pan or deep baking dish. Cover the beef with boiling water, add the beer and spices, cover, and place in the oven. Bake for 2½ hours or until the meat is tender when pierced with a fork (if necessary, add more water during baking in order to keep the meat covered). Remove the beef from the pan, place in a shallow baking dish, and set aside to cool.*

Combine the brown sugar and mustard in a small bowl and spread over the meat. Bake in a 400°F. oven for 30 minutes or until the glaze is bubbly and the meat is heated through. Cut the beef into thin slices and serve warm or at room temperature with rye and/or pumpernickel breads and assorted mustards.

At this point, the beef may be covered and stored in the refrigerator to be glazed at a later time.

Serves 16

Kaye Candler

Rizā-i Abbāsī Persian (Isfahan), active 1620-35, *Youth in Western Dress,* Safavid Dynasty, signed and dated 1634, tempera and ink on paper, 14.6 x 19.2 cm. Gift of Robert H. Tannahill in memory of Dr. Wilhelm R. Valentiner (58.334).

The Mayor's Favorite

This chili packs a punch!

½ cup butter or cooking oil
4 cloves garlic, minced
1½ cups onions, chopped
2 pounds ground beef
2 cups tomato sauce
2 cups water
1 8-ounce can tomatoes
1 cup green peppers, chopped
1 teaspoon celery seed
½ teaspoon cayenne pepper

2 teaspoons ground cumin seed
4 tablespoons chili powder (or to taste)
½ teaspoon dried basil
1 tablespoon salt

In a large saucepan, heat the butter or oil, add the garlic and onion, and sauté until golden. Add the beef and continue cooking until the meat has browned. Add the remaining ingredients to the pan and bring to a slow boil. Reduce the heat and simmer, uncovered, stirring occasionally until the mixture reaches the desired consistency (about 45 minutes). Adjust the seasonings and serve in large bowls.

Serves 6

Coleman A. Young

Breaded Veal Slices with Michigan Bing Cherries

A rich concoction, spicy and sweet —

1 16-ounce can Michigan Bing cherries, drained
¾ cup brandy
3 veal round steaks, cut into ¾-inch thick slices
Salt and pepper to taste
Paprika
Bread crumbs
1–2 eggs combined with 2 tablespoons water, beaten lightly
2 tablespoons butter
2 cups heavy cream

Add the cherries to the brandy and set aside to soak until needed. Wipe the veal with a damp cloth, trim, and pound well with a meat hammer or the edge of a plate. Score the veal lightly on both sides in a crisscross pattern, cut each slice into medallions the size of a large oyster, and season with salt, pepper, and paprika. Dip the veal in the bread crumbs, then in the beaten egg, and again in the crumbs.

Heat the butter in a skillet and brown the veal quickly on both sides. Pour the cream over the slices, cover, reduce the heat, and simmer for 15–30 minutes (or place the covered skillet in a 325°F. oven for 15–30 minutes). Place the meat and sauce on a serving platter and garnish with the brandy-soaked cherries.

Serves 4–6

Mrs. John B. Ford

Grilled Flank Steak with Red Wine and Shallot Sauce

From grill to table in under ten minutes; here's the clue to a perfect yet easy feast —

4 pounds flank steak
Soy sauce
Salt and freshly ground pepper to taste
1 teaspoon thyme
½ cup shallots or green onions, chopped
1¼ cups red wine
½ cup butter
2 tablespoons parsley, chopped

Brush the steak with the soy sauce and sprinkle with the salt, pepper, and thyme. Let the steak stand at room temperature for 1 hour, then brush with additional soy sauce, place over a brisk fire, and grill 3–4 minutes per side for rare (another minute or so per side for medium).

Combine the shallots or green onions and the wine in a small saucepan, and bring almost to a boil. Add the butter, stir until the butter has melted completely, and add the chopped parsley. Slice the steak on the diagonal and serve with the sauce.

Serves 8

Gayle Camden

Enchilada Puff Pie

An "elevated" version of the Mexican stand-by—

1½ pounds lean ground beef
1 cup (or more) onion, chopped
5 ounces tomato sauce
⅓ cup pitted, ripe olives, sliced
¼ cup water
2 teaspoons chili powder
1 teaspoon salt
1 teaspoon coriander
½ teaspoon cumin
¼ teaspoon cinnamon
6 eggs, separated
2 tablespoons flour
1 cup Cheddar cheese, shredded
2 cups corn chips, crushed coarsely
Paprika

Meissen Manufactory (Germany), modeled by Johann Joachim Kändler, German, 1706–1775, *Platter* from the *Swan Service*, 1737/41, porcelain, diam. 38.1 cm. Gift of Mr. and Mrs. James S. Whitcomb (57.29).

In a skillet, brown the meat and drain off the fat. Add the onion and sauté until transparent. Stir in the tomato sauce, olives, water, chili powder (add extra chili powder for a spicier flavor), ½ teaspoon of the salt, coriander, cumin, and cinnamon. Bring the mixture to a boil, reduce the heat, and keep warm.

In a small bowl, beat the egg whites until stiff and set aside. In a separate bowl, beat the yolks until thick and lemon-colored and blend in the flour and remaining salt. Lightly fold in the cheese and then the egg whites.

Cover the bottom of a 1½-quart casserole or soufflé dish with the crushed corn chips. Pour the beef mixture over the chips, cover with the egg mixture, and sprinkle with paprika. Bake in a 350°F. oven for 20–30 minutes or until the topping is puffed and golden.

Serves 4

Doris Burton

Stuffed Leg of Lamb

Vivo Italiano!

1 cup Italian dressing
3 onions, 1 sliced into rings and 2 chopped
1 leg of lamb, boned and trimmed of fat
5 tablespoons butter
4 cloves garlic, chopped
1 10-ounce package frozen spinach, chopped
1 cup Italian bread crumbs
Salt and pepper to taste
Lamb or chicken stock (optional)
½ teaspoon rosemary
Flour*

Combine the Italian dressing and the onion rings and marinate the leg of lamb in the refrigerator for 12 hours or overnight.

Melt the butter in a large frying pan, add the chopped onions and garlic, and cook until lightly browned. In a separate pan, cook the spinach as directed, drain, and squeeze dry. Combine the spinach with the chopped onions and the bread crumbs and add salt and pepper to taste.

Preheat the oven to 475°F. Remove the lamb from the marinade and pat dry. Spread the spinach stuffing in the center of the lamb, bring up the sides, and skewer or tie with cook's twine to make a neat roll. Put the lamb in a roasting pan, skin side up, rub all over with butter, and place in the oven for 15 minutes. Reduce the heat to 325°F. and cook the lamb for

1¾ hours more.

When the lamb is done, gravy may be made by skimming off any fat from the lamb juices, adding a little lamb or chicken stock and ½ teaspoon of rosemary, and blending with flour to reach the desired consistency.

**Wondra Flour is recommended to achieve the best consistency.*
Serves 8

Jeanette Keramedjian

Nigerian Bachelor's Stew

Exotic and spicy —

3 ripe tomatoes, peeled, seeded, and chopped
2 sweet red peppers, chopped
1 small hot green pepper, chopped (or ½
    teaspoon dried hot pepper)
1 large yellow onion, chopped
¼ cup palm oil (or ¼ cup vegetable oil
    combined with ½ teaspoon sesame oil)
1–2 cups water
2 tablespoons tomato paste
½ teaspoon basil
Salt, pepper, and additional hot pepper to
    taste
2 chicken breasts, skinned, boned, and cut
    into 1-inch squares*
3 eggs, beaten
Hot, cooked rice (or boiled white yams)

In a large skillet, sauté the tomatoes, peppers, and onion in the palm oil until translucent, add ¼ cup of water and the tomato paste, and cook over medium to high heat until the mixture boils actively. Continue to add water ¼ cup at a time over the next 30 minutes or until the tomatoes lose their sweetness. Add seasonings to taste.

Add the chicken to the pan, stir to coat, reduce the heat, cover, and cook for 4–5 minutes. Remove the cover, add the eggs, let sit for 30 seconds until the eggs are slightly set, and stir gently. Cook until the eggs are fully set and the stew has thickened. Serve over steamed white rice or boiled white yams.

In lieu of the chicken, try ½ pound of peeled and deveined shrimp or ½ pound of boiled stew beef, cut into 1-inch squares. Both make excellent variations!

Serves 4

David Penney

African (Yoruba), *Kola Nut Container*, 19th/20th cent., wood and indigo, h. with cover 29.2 cm; diam. at base 20 cm. Gift of the Honorable and Mrs. G. Mennen Williams (74.45).

Osso Buco

Gremolata, a rich and flavorful lemon-herb sauce, perfectly complements these Italian-style, braised veal shanks.

6 pounds veal shanks, cut into 2-inch
    lengths
Salt and pepper to taste
Nutmeg to taste
Flour
1 medium carrot, pared and shredded
1 large onion, minced
4 cloves garlic, minced
1 1-pound can tomatoes, chopped coarsely
    (reserve liquid)
½ cup dry white wine
1 tablespoon salt
1 teaspoon sugar
½ teaspoon thyme
¼ teaspoon sage

⅓ cup fresh parsley, minced
1 tablespoon lemon rind, grated

Preheat the oven to 325°F. Sprinkle the veal with salt, pepper, and a pinch of nutmeg, coat lightly with the flour, and place in a roasting pan with the carrot and onion and 2 cloves of the garlic. Combine the tomatoes, tomato liquid, wine, salt, sugar, thyme, and sage and pour into the pan. Cover and bake for 1¼–1½ hours or until the veal is tender, stirring once or twice.

To prepare *gremolata*, combine the remaining garlic, the parsley, and the lemon rind and set aside. Remove the veal to a warm serving dish and pour the cooking liquid into a large skillet. Bring the liquid to a boil and cook, stirring constantly, until thickened. Stir in one-half of the parsley mixture, pour the sauce over the veal, and sprinkle the remaining parsley over the top.

Serves 6

Lee Frank

Cousin Jacks

Pasties, brought to Michigan around 1850 by Cornish miners, were later adapted by the Finns. Recipes such as this one have been handed down from generation to generation.

3 cups unbleached, all-purpose flour
1½–2 teaspoons salt
1½ teaspoons baking powder
⅔ cup lard
½ cup suet
⅓ cup cold water (or as needed)
1 medium onion, diced
3 medium boiling potatoes, peeled and diced
3 carrots or 1 cup rutabaga, peeled and diced
¾ pound beef chuck, chopped coarsely
¼ pound pork loin, chopped coarsely
Pepper to taste
Butter

Sift together the flour, 1½ teaspoons of the salt, and the baking powder. Cut the lard and suet into the flour mixture with a fork or in a food processor until the dough resembles coarse meal. Stir in just enough cold water so that the dough almost pulls together in a mass, wrap, and chill for 1 hour.

Preheat the oven to 425°F. Remove the dough from the refrigerator and let stand a few minutes before using. Mix together the vegetables and meats in a large bowl, season to taste with pepper and the remaining salt, and set aside.

When the dough has chilled, divide into 6 pieces and roll each on a lightly floured surface to form circles 6½–7½ inches in diameter. Trim the edges using an inverted plate as a pattern. Place ⅙ of the filling in the center of each pastry circle and dot with butter. Brush the edges of the pastry with cold water, fold the dough over to form a semicircle, and crimp the edges firmly. The pasty should look like a bulging half-moon. Continue until six pasties have been formed.*

Bake the pastries on a greased cookie sheet for 10-12 minutes or until they begin to brown. Reduce the heat to 350°F. and continue baking another 50 minutes or until they are golden brown and bubbling hot. The pastries may be served hot or warm.

The pasties may be prepared in advance to this point and frozen.

Serves 6

Lynn W. Day

Golabki

Authentic Polish cabbage rolls filled with meat and rice —

1 head cabbage (approximately 4 pounds)
6 quarts boiling, salted water
1 onion, chopped
2 tablespoons oil
1½ pounds ground beef
½ pound ground pork
1½ cups raw rice, cooked
1 teaspoon salt
¼ teaspoon pepper
1 10-ounce can tomato soup
5 ounces tomato catsup
2½ cups water

Preheat the oven to 350°F. Remove the core from the cabbage, place it in the boiling, salted water, cover, and cook for 3 minutes or until soft enough to remove the large outer leaves (there should be about 20). Shave the thick stem from each leaf and set the leaves aside. Chop the remaining cabbage and set aside.

In a skillet, sauté the onion in the oil and add the meats, rice, salt, and pepper, mixing thoroughly. Place a heaping tablespoon of the meat mixture on each leaf, tuck the sides over the filling, roll up, and secure with a toothpick. Place half of the chopped cabbage in the bottom of a large Dutch oven, fill with a layer of cabbage rolls, and cover with the remaining chopped cabbage.

Combine the tomato soup and catsup with the water, mix until smooth, and pour over the cabbage. Cover and bake until the mixture bubbles, reduce the heat to 300°F., and bake for 1½ hours. Serve the cabbage rolls topped with the tomato sauce.

Note: As a variation, try the spicy *Tomato Sauce* on p. 119.

Serves 10

Zofia Drozdowska-Kafarski

American, *High Chest of Drawers*, 1760/90, walnut, 245.8 x 114.3 x 57.5 cm. Robert H. Tannahill Foundation and Henry Ford II Funds (73.3).

Stuffed Veal

Tender and tempting —

1 4-*pound veal shoulder, trimmed of bone and cartilage*
10 *slices white bread*
1 *small and* 1 *medium onion, minced (keep separate)*
½ *cup butter*
1 *cup watercress, minced*
6 *sprigs parsley, minced*
1 *teaspoon salt*
½ *teaspoon rosemary*
¼ *teaspoon freshly ground pepper*
2 *carrots, minced*
2 *stalks celery, diced*
1 *cup beef consommé*

Flatten the meat to form a rectangle approximately ½-inch thick and set aside. Place the bread slices in a blender or food processor, process into fine crumbs, and set aside.

In a skillet, sauté the small chopped onion in the butter. Transfer to a small bowl, add the bread crumbs, watercress, and seasonings, and mix thoroughly.

Spread the stuffing evenly over the flattened veal shoulder. Starting at either end of the rectangle, roll the meat and tie securely in several places with cook's twine or soft cord.

In the bottom of a baking pan combine the carrots, celery, and medium onion. Place the veal roll on top of the vegetables and add the beef consommé. Cover the pan, bake at 350°F. for 1 hour, remove the cover, and bake an additional 30 minutes. Transfer the veal to a plate, remove the strings, and slice thinly. Serve hot with gravy on the side or chilled.

Serves 6

Vi Reghanti

Breast of Lamb

Succulent lamb on a bed of herbed rice —

2 *boneless breasts of lamb (or 1 large breast with bones)*
2 *tablespoons butter*
1 *large onion, chopped*
1 *teaspoon Fines Herbes*
½ *cup raw rice*
1 *cup chicken broth (made from concentrate)*
½ *cup parsley, chopped*
Salt and pepper to taste
1 *cup white wine*

Preheat the oven to 450°F. Trim the fat from the lamb breasts, make a pocket in each, and set aside. Melt the butter in a heavy pan, add the onion, and sauté for 2 minutes. Add the herbs and rice and stir to coat. Stir in the chicken broth, bring the mixture to a boil, and cover. Reduce the heat, cook for 8 minutes, remove from the heat, and let stand until the rice has absorbed all of the liquid. Stir in the parsley.

Stuff the breasts with the rice mixture and sew the pockets closed with strong thread. Season with salt and pepper to taste, place in the oven, and roast for 10 minutes. Lower the heat to 350°F., roast for 30 minutes more, baste, and roast an additional 15 minutes. Add the white wine to the cooking juices and baste the breasts every 15 minutes for the next hour (approximately 2 hours total cooking time). Remove the breasts from the oven and take out the stitches before slicing. Skim as much fat as possible from the juices and serve on the side.

Serves 6

Leneda Maki

Lamb Curry

Morsels of tender lamb steeped in aromatic spices —

¼ cup butter
3 medium onions, chopped
1 carrot, chopped
1 stalk celery, chopped
½ green pepper, seeded and chopped
2 tablespoons parsley, minced
2 tablespoons flour
1½ cups beef or chicken stock
½ cup dry red or white wine
½ cup tomato, chopped
½ cup coconut milk
¼ cup lime juice
3 tablespoons chutney
2½ tablespoons brown sugar
2 tablespoons golden raisins
Bouquet Garni (or 2 whole cloves and
   1 small bay leaf tied in cheesecloth)
1–3 teaspoons curry powder, moistened with
   cold water
½ teaspoon cinnamon
½ teaspoon cumin
⅛ teaspoon nutmeg
Salt and freshly ground pepper
3 cups cooked lean lamb, cubed
2 large tart apples, peeled, cored, and cubed
¼ cup plain yogurt or sour cream
Rice, cooked

In a large saucepan, melt the butter over medium heat. Add the onion, carrot, celery, green pepper, and parsley and sauté until the onion is golden. In a small bowl, combine the flour with a little stock, stirring until the flour dissolves, and add to the sautéed vegetables, blending thoroughly. Stir in the remaining stock, wine, and tomato and simmer for 5 minutes.

Add the coconut milk, lime juice, chutney, brown sugar, raisins, Bouquet Garni, spices, salt, and pepper and simmer for 20 minutes. Add the lamb, cook 15 minutes more,* then gently stir in the apples and yogurt. Serve the lamb curry in the center of a rice ring or on a platter with rice and condiments.

*The curry may be prepared in advance to this point and refrigerated or frozen. Add the apple and yogurt just before the curry is reheated.

Note: The curry sauce is also very good with leftover beef or poultry.
   Serves 6

Junia Doan

Lamb Shanks with Orzo and Feta

Tangy feta distinguishes this gift from the Greeks.

3 pounds lamb shanks
¼ cup vegetable oil
1 cup onion, chopped
1 teaspoon rosemary, chopped
1 bay leaf
2–2½ cups chicken stock
½ cup fresh lemon juice
2 tablespoons lemon peel, cut into julienne
   strips
½ cup orzo
¾ cup feta cheese, crumbled
¼ cup parsley, chopped

Preheat the oven to 325°F. In a large, heavy casserole, brown the lamb shanks in the oil and transfer to a platter. In the remaining oil, sauté the onions over low heat until wilted. Return the lamb to the casserole, add the herbs and the chicken stock, and bake for 2–2½ hours or until the lamb is tender. Remove the lamb from the oven, let stand to cool, remove the meat from the bones, and set aside.

Add the lemon juice and peel to the cooking broth and reduce to 1½–2 cups over high heat. In a saucepan of boiling water, cook the orzo for 8 minutes, drain, and rinse in cold water. Return the meat and orzo to the reduced cooking liquid, stir in the feta cheese, and add a little more lemon juice or chicken stock if needed. Simmer just until the lamb and orzo are heated through. Sprinkle with parsley and serve.
   Serves 4–6

Susanne Hilberry

CONDIMENTS AND DRESSINGS

*C*ondiments are many times overshadowed by the more substantial offerings at mealtime. However, they quite often save a left-over bit of beef or commonplace chicken from oblivion. Similarly, salad dressings are considered secondary to the contents of a salad, while the reverse is often true; it is quite possible that some salads were created solely to complement the dressings they are graced with. Whether they are served in elegant vessels, such as the early nineteenth-century silver *Sauceboat and Stand,* or with an intricately carved ivory *Spoon* from Africa, the recipes in this section offer a variety of flavors to enhance every aspect of your meal.

Perhaps we have come to associate condiments more with meals *en plein air,* or picnics. Condiments and picnics go together just as do picnics and beautiful, sun-filled hours near the water. A more perfect day than that depicted in *Promenade,* by Maurice Prendergast, could hardly be imagined, nor a better pastime than a picnic and a stroll along the shores of Michigan's waterways.

Maurice Prendergast, American, 1859-1924, *Promenade* (detail), 1914/15, oil on canvas, 212.7 x 340.4 cm. City of Detroit Purchase (27.159).

Marinated Carrots

An intriguing flavor —

1 pound small carrots
2 bay leaves
3 tablespoons sugar
½ cup white vinegar
¼ cup water
1 clove garlic, crushed
½ teaspoon each salt, mustard seed, dill
    weed, dill seed, and crushed red pepper

Steam or parboil the carrots for 12–15 minutes or until they are barely tender. Plunge them into cold water and rub or scrape off the skins. Pack the carrots into a pint jar and add the bay leaves.

Combine the remaining ingredients in a small saucepan and place over low heat, stirring just long enough to blend and dissolve the sugar. Pour the mixture over the carrots and bay leaves, seal the jar, and refrigerate for at least 2 days before serving.

Note: *Marinated Carrots* will keep in the refrigerator for up to 3 weeks.

Yields 1 pint

Delphine J. Andrews

Pickled Beets

A refreshing side dish —

2 pounds beets, boiled until tender and
    drained (or the equivalent of canned,
    sliced beets)
⅔ cup sugar
1 teaspoon allspice
½ teaspoon salt
2 tablespoons cider vinegar
½ cup water
½ stick cinnamon

Peel and slice the beets, place in a 1-quart jar, and set aside. Combine the remaining ingredients in a saucepan and simmer for 15 minutes. Remove the cinnamon stick, pour the hot mixture over the beets, cap the jar tightly, and store in the refrigerator for several days before serving.

Yields 1 quart

Bea Wells

Madeira Sauce

Best with a rare filet of beef —

3 tablespoons butter
3 tablespoons shallots, minced
⅓ cup Madeira
1 10¾-ounce can consommé
4 teaspoons cornstarch
1 teaspoon cold water (approximately)
½ cup mushrooms, sautéed (optional)

In a saucepan, melt the butter, add the shallots, and cook until soft. Add the Madeira and the consommé and blend well. Mix the cornstarch with the cold water, whisk into the sauce, and simmer for 20 minutes. Sautéed mushrooms may be added just before serving.

Yields approximately 1½ cups

The Cookbook Committee

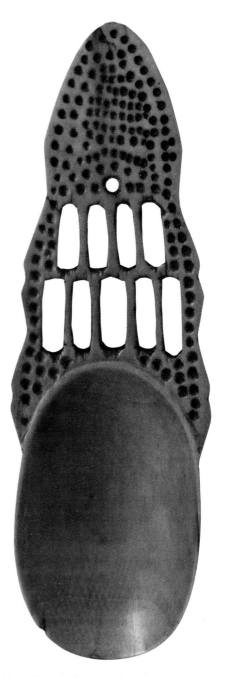

African (Lega), *Spoon*, n.d.a., ivory, 20 x 6.7 cm. Bequest of Robert H. Tannahill (70.42).

Dilled Green Tomatoes

An excellent way to use the last of summer's small green tomatoes —

2 quarts small green tomatoes
2 cups white vinegar
2 cups water
¼ cup salt
2 small onions, diced
½ green pepper, diced
2 stalks celery, chopped

1 clove garlic, minced
1 bunch fresh dill

Wash and drain the tomatoes. In a large pan, combine the vinegar, water, and salt, bring to a boil, and cook for 5 minutes. Pack the tomatoes in two sterilized, 1-quart jars, add the onion, pepper, celery, and garlic, and place the fresh dill on top. Pour the boiling vinegar mixture over all, seal the jars, and process in a hot-water bath. Do not open for 6 weeks.
Yields 2 quarts

The Cookbook Committee

Tomato Sauce

Serves a multitude of purposes —

2 large onions, chopped
½ cup olive oil
2 cloves garlic
2 large stalks celery, chopped
2 green peppers, chopped
2 quarts tomatoes, peeled and chopped
2 6-ounce cans tomato paste
1 cup beef broth
2 bay leaves
2 teaspoons basil
1 teaspoon thyme
2 teaspoons oregano

½ cup fresh parsley, chopped
Salt and pepper to taste
½ teaspoon sugar (or to taste)

In a saucepan, sauté the onions in the oil, add the remaining ingredients, and simmer uncovered for 1 hour. Put the sauce through a food mill or processor before serving.
Note: This sauce freezes well: after processing, pour into 1-cup plastic freezerware dishes or into muffin tins and freeze. (If muffin tins are used, each frozen "round" of sauce will equal approximately ⅓ cup — remove the rounds when frozen and store in plastic bags.)
Yields 12 cups

The Cookbook Committee

Sally Nieman's Corn Relish

An old family recipe —

1 dozen ears fresh, ripe corn
4 cups onions, chopped coarsely
3 green peppers, chopped coarsely
4 cups cucumbers, peeled and chopped
  coarsely
4 cups tomatoes, skinned and chopped
  coarsely
8 small, hot red peppers, chopped coarsely
2 cups sugar

⅓ cup salt
2 cups white vinegar
2 tablespoons mustard seed
1 tablespoon turmeric

Remove the corn from the cobs and combine with the remaining ingredients in a large kettle. Bring to a boil, reduce the heat, and simmer for 30 minutes, stirring often. Pour into eight hot, sterilized pint jars and seal with sterilized rings and caps. Carefully wipe the top of each jar to help assure a good seal. Process the relish in a hot water bath.
Yields 8 pints

Ruth Holcomb

Michigan Peach Chutney

A native interpretation of the East Indian condiment —

½ cup onions, chopped
½ pound seedless raisins
1 clove garlic, minced
4 pounds firm, Michigan peaches, peeled,
    stoned, and chopped
¾ cup preserved stem ginger (or to taste)
2 tablespoons mustard seed, crushed
1 tablespoon chili powder

1½ teaspoons salt
1 quart vinegar
1–1¼ pounds brown sugar

In a large, enameled pan, combine all of the ingredients, bring to a boil, and simmer for 1 hour or until the mixture has thickened. Pour the chutney into sterilized jars and seal at once.
    Note: Preserved stem ginger may be found in specialty food stores.
    Yields 3 pints

The Cookbook Committee

Cranberry Fruit Conserve

Serve this tart mixture with the holiday turkey.

1 pound fresh cranberries, washed and
    drained
1½ cups water
2½ cups sugar
1 cup white raisins, chopped
1 apple, peeled, cored, and chopped
Juice and grated rind of 1 orange

Juice and grated rind of 1 lemon
1 cup walnuts, chopped

In a large pan, combine the cranberries and water and cook until the skins of the berries pop open. Add the sugar, raisins, apple, and orange and lemon juices and rinds, bring to a boil, and cook for 15 minutes. Remove the pan from the heat, add the walnuts, and stir to blend. Pour the mixture into two hot, sterilized pint jars and seal with sterilized rings and caps.
    Yields approximately 2 pints

Loris Birnkrant

Marquand & Co., American, *Sauceboat and Stand*, 1833/39, silver, 16.2 x 10.8 x 19 cm (sauceboat), 3.2 x 18.4 x 27.3 cm (stand). Founders Society Purchase with funds from Mr. and Mrs. Alan W. Joslyn in memory of Robert H. Tannahill (71.4 a,b).

Cumberland Sauce

Hot or cold, it distinguishes most meats and poultry.

1 tablespoon shallots, minced
Rind of 1 lemon, cut into julienne strips
Rind of 1 orange, cut into julienne strips
Juice of ½ lemon
Juice of 1 orange
¾ cup red currant jelly, melted
⅔ cup port
1 teaspoon Dijon mustard
1 teaspoon fresh ginger, grated (or ½
    teaspoon ground ginger)
Pinch of cayenne pepper

Place the shallots, lemon and orange rinds, and lemon and orange juices in a saucepan and simmer for 10 minutes. Add the currant jelly, port, mustard, ginger, and cayenne pepper, mix well, and bring back to a simmer, stirring constantly. Serve the sauce hot or at room temperature.
    Note: *Cumberland Sauce* is best served hot with game, chicken, or ham or cold with pâté.
    Yields approximately 1½ cups

The Cookbook Committee

Jean-François Millet, French, 1814–1875, *Mother Feeding Her Children*, n.d.a., pastel and chalk, 34.8 x 28.6 cm. Gift of Mrs. Joseph B. Schlotman (73.104).

Henry's Dressing

A vinaigrette with the flavor of Dijon —

1 cup olive oil
4 tablespoons red wine vinegar
2 tablespoons white or cider vinegar
1 teaspoon Dijon mustard
1 teaspoon sugar (optional)
Dash of Worcestershire sauce
Salt and pepper to taste
½ teaspoon each garlic and onion, minced
½ teaspoon parsley, thyme, or oregano

Combine all of the ingredients in a covered jar and shake well. The dressing may be stored in the refrigerator for several weeks and shaken prior to using.
    Yields 1½ cups

Henry Ford II

Hot Barbecue Sauce

Summer in the city, Detroit style —

2 cups catsup
½ cup vinegar
½ cup butter
6 tablespoons Worcestershire sauce
Juice of 4 lemons
1 clove garlic, minced
1 tablespoon dry mustard
2 teaspoons Tabasco sauce
½ tablespoon onion salt
1 teaspoon pepper

In a saucepan, combine all of the ingredients and cook over low heat until the butter has melted. Raise the heat, bring to a boil, and cook for 1 minute, stirring to blend well.
    Note: *Hot Barbecue Sauce* may be stored in the refrigerator for up to one month.
    Yields approximately 4 cups

The Cookbook Committee

Schuss Mountain Mustard Sauce

The best match for ham or boiled beef —

2 eggs, beaten well
½ cup granulated or brown sugar
4 tablespoons dry mustard
½ cup cider vinegar
½ cup milk
1 tablespoon butter

In a saucepan over low heat, combine all of the ingredients, bring to a slow boil, and cook, stirring until thickened.

Yields 1½ cups

Trudi Wineman

Homemade Mayonnaise

Simple, smooth, and a perfect complement to many foods —

1 egg
2 tablespoons lemon juice
¼ teaspoon salt
¼ teaspoon dry mustard
1 cup vegetable oil

In a blender, combine the egg, lemon juice, salt, mustard, and ¼ cup of the

vegetable oil and blend on low speed. While blending, slowly add the remaining oil and process until smooth. Refrigerate immediately.

Yields 1¼ cups

The Cookbook Committee

Patrice's French Dressing

A creamy version of the classic mustard vinaigrette —

3 tablespoons Balsamic red wine vinegar
½ cup olive oil
1 teaspoon Dijon mustard
2 tablespoons shallots, minced
Salt and pepper to taste
1–2 teaspoons heavy cream

Add the olive oil to the vinegar in a slow stream while whisking briskly. Blend in the mustard and shallots and season to taste with salt and pepper. Gradually add the cream and whisk until smooth.

Yields ¾ cup

Patrice Marandel

Tiffany and Company, American, *Ewer*, ca. 1893, sterling silver, h. 44.8 cm. Founders Society Purchase with funds from Mr. and Mrs. Charles Theron Van Dusen in memory of Charles Theron Van Dusen (1984.6).

Egg Vinaigrette

This flavorful dressing will transform any salad.

1 cup vinegar
¼ cup salad or olive oil
½ cup mayonnaise
¼ teaspoon salt
¼ teaspoon garlic powder
1½ teaspoons prepared mustard

2 eggs, hard-boiled and minced
3 tablespoons chives, chopped

In a small bowl, slowly add the vinegar to the oil. Stir in the mayonnaise and blend well. Season the mixture with salt,

garlic powder, and mustard. Add the eggs and chives, mix well, and chill thoroughly before serving.

Yields 1½ cups

Raquel Ross

Cleo's Seasoned Greetings

The creator of this wonderful seasoning, which is especially good in salad dressings, gave it to friends each Christmas.

12 or more cloves garlic
3 cups Kosher salt
¼ cup paprika
3 tablespoons black pepper
2 tablespoons dried basil

2 tablespoons dried parsley
½ cup Accent (optional)

Mash the garlic cloves and the salt with a mortar and pestle. Add the remaining ingredients and mix well. Store the seasoning in air-tight jars in the refrigerator.

Yields 4 cups

Cleo Gruber

Sauce Verte

Especially good with cold, poached salmon —

4 bunches watercress
1 10-ounce bag spinach
4 teaspoons dried dill weed
　　(or 2 tablespoons fresh dill)
Juice of 1 lemon

2 cups mayonnaise
1 cup sour cream

Wash the greens, snip off and discard any large stems, pat dry, and chop finely or process in a food processor. Add the remaining ingredients, mix thoroughly, and refrigerate at least 2 hours to blend the flavors.

Yields 4 cups

Lois Mack

Butterscotch Sauce

A rich, buttery topping for cakes or ice cream —

1 cup light brown sugar, packed firmly
4 tablespoons sweet butter, cut into small
　　pieces
¼ cup water
¼ cup light corn syrup
½ cup heavy cream
1 teaspoon vanilla

Combine the brown sugar, butter, water, and corn syrup in a heavy saucepan and cook over medium heat, stirring constantly, until the sugar has completely dissolved. Bring the mixture to a boil, insert a candy thermometer, and cook over moderately high heat, without stirring, until the temperature on the candy thermometer registers 240°F.

Remove the pan from the heat, add the cream, and return to a boil for 2 minutes. Remove from the heat again and stir in the vanilla. Serve the sauce warm or at room temperature.

Note: *Butterscotch Sauce* may be covered and stored in the refrigerator for up to a month.

Yields 1½ cups

The Cookbook Committee

Hot Chocolate Fudge Sauce

Bittersweet and very rich —

6 tablespoons sweet butter
6 ounces unsweetened baking chocolate
1 cup boiling water
1¾ cups sugar
½ cup light corn syrup
Dash of salt
1 teaspoon vanilla

Combine the butter and the chocolate in a heavy saucepan and stir over low heat until completely melted. Stir in the water, sugar, corn syrup, and salt. Bring the mixture to a boil and, without stirring, maintain the boil for 8–10 minutes or until the mixture has thickened. Remove the pan from the heat and stir in the vanilla. The sauce is best served hot.

Note: *Hot Chocolate Fudge Sauce* may be stored in the refrigerator for months. To reheat, place the sauce in the top of a double boiler and stir until heated through.

Yields approximately 2 cups

Joy Emery

BREADS
AND COFFEE CAKES

*B*read, in its many forms, is considered one of life's most basic necessities. The rudiments of bread-making have come down to us from ancient times and with them an understanding of the continuum of time and tradition. In fact, the age-old custom of "breaking bread together" is still symbolic of a collective humanity that must share the same nourishment to survive.

Breads have been depicted in art not only as a symbol of sustenance but for their simple shapes and rich textures. This still life by twentieth-century French artist Auguste Herbin juxtaposes the somber color and texture of a loaf of bread with the vivid orange of fruit and the smooth surface of a table to create a scene of domestic simplicity. Similarly, American artist Raphaelle Peale's *Still Life with Wine Glass* makes use of the squat, round form of a hard roll and the split, grainy surfaces of muffins to contrast with the smoothness of the wine glass and plate and the crinkled skins of the fruit.

Presented here are generations-old recipes for whole-grain breads and muffins as well as luscious, aromatic coffee cakes that will be equally at home on holiday tables, gracing the breakfast or brunch table, or accompanying coffee and tea in the late afternoon.

Auguste Herbin, French, 1882–1960, *Still Life* (detail), 20th cent., oil on canvas, 54 x 64.8 cm. City of Detroit Purchase (26.35).

Round French Bread

Especially suited to those leery of making yeast breads —

1 envelope yeast
1 tablespoon sugar
1½–2 cups water, heated to 115° F.
2 teaspoons salt
4–4½ cups bread flour
1 tablespoon butter, melted

In a large bowl, lightly stir the yeast and sugar into the warm water and set aside. When the mixture bubbles, stir in the salt, 4 cups of the flour, and enough additional warm water (about ½ cup) to make a soft dough. Knead on a floured board, adding additional flour as necessary, until the dough is no longer sticky. Transfer to a large, greased bowl, cover, and let rise in a warm place.

When the dough has doubled in size, punch it down, divide into two portions, and place each in a greased, 6-inch casserole. Cover loosely and let rise until the dough reaches the top of the casseroles.

Preheat the oven to 350° F., brush the tops of the loaves with melted butter, and bake for 45 minutes. Cool on racks before slicing.

Yields 2 loaves

Cynthia Jo Fogliatti

Gloria's Roman Garlic Bread

The only suitable companion to an Italian meal!

½ cup butter, softened
½ teaspoon garlic salt
3 teaspoons parsley, chopped
½ teaspoon oregano
2 tablespoons Parmesan cheese, grated
4 tablespoons sour cream
1 loaf of bread

Preheat the oven to 400° F. Combine the butter, garlic salt, parsley, oregano, cheese, and sour cream and let stand at room temperature for 30 minutes. Slice the bread, spread the top and both sides of each slice with the Parmesan mixture, and reassemble in loaf form. Wrap the bread in foil,* bake for 10 minutes, unwrap, and bake for an additional 5 minutes. Serve immediately.

The bread may be prepared in advance to this point and refrigerated for up to 24 hours.

Yields 1 loaf

Trudi Wineman

Bran Muffins

The breakfast table staple —

1½ cups all-bran cereal
1¼ cups 2-percent milk
1½ cups all-purpose, unbleached flour
2½ teaspoons baking powder
1 teaspoon salt
¼ cup corn oil
⅓ cup sugar
¼ cup dark molasses
1 egg
1 cup raisins
1 cup pecans or walnuts, broken into pieces
2 tablespoons orange zest, slivered finely

Preheat the oven to 400° F. Combine the bran and milk and let stand at room temperature for 5–10 minutes. Sift the flour, baking powder, and salt together and set aside.

Combine the oil and sugar, blend in the molasses, egg, raisins, nuts, and orange zest, and fold in the bran mixture.* Gradually add the dry ingredients, mixing just until they are blended. Fill greased muffin cups two-thirds full and bake for 25–35 minutes.

Approximately 2–3 tablespoons of unprocessed bran cereal may be added for a crunchier texture.

Yields 12

Virginia Johnston

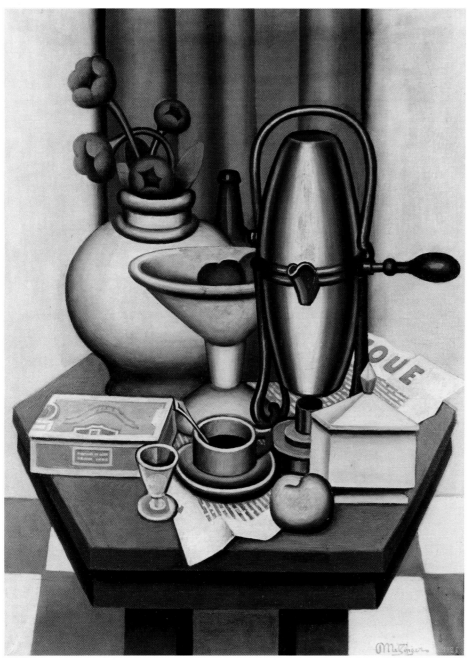

Gougères

One word describes these — heavenly!

1 cup water
6 tablespoons butter
1 teaspoon salt
⅛ teaspoon pepper
1 cup flour
4 large eggs
1 teaspoon Dijon mustard
1 teaspoon dry mustard
1 pinch nutmeg
1 cup Swiss or Gruyère cheese, grated

Preheat the oven to 475°F. Grease a baking sheet, cover with parchment paper, and set aside.

In a heavy saucepan, combine the water, butter, salt, and pepper and bring to a boil. Add the flour and stir until the mixture leaves the sides of the pan and forms a ball. Remove the pan from the heat, add the eggs one at a time, beating well, and stir in the mustards, nutmeg, and all but a few spoonfuls of the cheese.

Drop scant teaspoonfuls of the dough on the baking sheet and sprinkle with the reserved cheese. Bake for approximately 25 minutes, remove from the oven, and slit the top of each roll to let the steam escape. Cool slightly on a wire rack before serving.

Note: The rolls may be frozen and reheated for 15 minutes in a 350°F. oven before serving.

Yields 2 dozen

Gayle Camden

Jean Metzinger, French, 1883-1956, *Still Life*, 1925, oil on canvas, 81 x 60 cm. Gift of Mr. and Mrs. Isadore Levin (57.238).

Blueberry Muffins

These light-textured muffins are perfect every time.

½ cup sugar
¼ cup butter, softened
1 egg
½ cup milk
1½ cups flour
2 teaspoons baking powder
½ teaspoon salt
1 cup fresh Michigan blueberries

Preheat the oven to 400°F. Grease muffin tins or line with paper baking cups and set aside.

In a large bowl, cream together the sugar and butter, add the egg and milk alternately with the flour, baking powder, and salt, and blend thoroughly. Gently fold in the blueberries, spoon into the muffin cups, and bake for 20–25 minutes or until lightly browned.
Yields 12

Ruth Holcomb

Poppy Seed Bread

A Polish favorite perfect for any meal —

4 eggs
2 cups sugar
1 13-ounce can evaporated milk
1½ cups salad oil
3 cups flour
4 teaspoons baking powder
½ teaspoon salt
½ cup poppy seeds

Preheat the oven to 350°F. In a large bowl, combine the eggs and sugar, add the milk and salad oil alternately with the dry ingredients, and blend thoroughly. Stir in the poppy seeds and pour the batter into two greased loaf pans. Bake for 50–60 minutes or until lightly browned and springy to the touch.
Yields 2 loaves

Lucie Kelly

Mexican (Vera Cruz), *Palma with Maize God Receiving a Human Sacrifice,* A.D.400–700, basalt, h. 48.3 cm. City of Detroit Purchase (47.180).

Indian Fry Bread

These small pillows of bread originated in Peshawbestown near Leland, Michigan. They should be light as a cloud and are delicious served as hors d'oeuvres or with soup or salad.

2 cups bread flour
2 teaspoons baking powder
1 teaspoon salt (or seasoned salt*)
½ teaspoon sugar
⅔ cup ice water
Oil for deep frying

In a mixing bowl, combine the flour, baking powder, salt, and sugar, and add only enough water to make a soft dough. Knead on a lightly floured board just un-til the dough is smooth, cover, and let rest for 20 minutes. Roll the dough into a rectangle approximately ¼-inch thick and cut into 2- or 3-inch squares.

Pour 2 inches of oil in a wok or deep frying pan and heat to 350–375°F. Working with a few squares of dough at a time, pull or stretch the squares slightly so as to maintain a uniform thinness and drop into the hot oil. Turn the squares frequently so that they puff and brown evenly, remove from the oil when golden, and drain on paper towels. Serve with butter and/or jam.

Seasoned salt is recommended if served as hors d'oeuvres.

Yields approximately 2 dozen

Frederick King W. Day

Honey Wheat Bread with Millet

A truly "down home" taste —

1½ cups water
1 cup small-curd cottage cheese
¼ cup honey
¼ cup butter
2 tablespoons sugar
1 tablespoon salt
2 packages dry yeast
⅓ cup millet*
2 cups whole wheat flour
4½–5 cups bread flour

In a saucepan, combine the water, cottage cheese, honey, and butter, insert a candy thermometer into the pan, and heat until the thermometer registers 120–130°F.

In a medium bowl, combine the sugar, salt, yeast, millet, and whole wheat flour, add the cottage cheese mixture, and beat for 2 minutes with an electric mixer. Stir in as much of the bread flour as possible, blend thoroughly, and turn the dough out onto a floured board.

Knead in additional bread flour as necessary (at least 4½ cups) until the dough is smooth and elastic. Form the dough into a ball and place in a large bowl which has been greased with butter or a non-stick spray. Coat a piece of plastic wrap with non-stick spray, cover the bowl, and put in a warm place until doubled in size (1–1½ hours) or until an indentation remains in the dough when touched.

Return the dough to the floured board, cut in half, and shape into 2 loaves. Place the loaves in 2 greased 9- by 5-inch pans, cover with plastic wrap, and return to a warm place to rise. Heat the oven to 350°F., bake the loaves for 45 minutes, turn out onto a wire rack, and cool completely before cutting.

Millet may be found at most health food stores.

Note: The following are two easy and very tasty variations of this recipe.

Onion Dill Bread: Increase the water by 3 tablespoons and substitute 3 tablespoons of instant onion flakes and 2 tablespoons of dill seed for the millet.

Herb Bread: Add 3 tablespoons of chicken stock base to the water and add 1 teaspoon each thyme, summer savory, and rosemary to the flour mixture.

Yields 2 loaves

Margie Gillis

Jeannie's Rugalach

Golden treats of cinnamon and currants —

1 pound sweet butter, softened
½ pound cream cheese, softened
3 tablespoons sour cream
3½–3⅔ cups flour
½ teaspoon salt
¾ cup granulated sugar
½ cup brown sugar
1½ teaspoons cinnamon
1 cup nuts, chopped .
½ cup currants (or golden raisins, chopped; optional)

In a large bowl, cream together the butter, cream cheese, and sour cream. Combine the flour, salt, and ¼ cup of the sugar, add to the butter mixture a little at a time, and blend thoroughly — the dough will be sticky. Wrap and refrigerate for several hours or overnight. In a small bowl, combine the remaining granulated sugar, the brown sugar, cinnamon, nuts, and currants or raisins and set aside.

Preheat the oven to 375°F. Divide the dough into 6 portions and, working with one portion at a time on a floured board, roll the dough into a 9-inch circle and cut the circle into 8 pie-shaped wedges. Sprinkle the filling over the dough and roll up each wedge, beginning with the widest edge, as if for a crescent roll. Place the rolls seam side down on a greased baking sheet and bake for 15 minutes or until lightly browned.

Yields approximately 4 dozen

Florence Schreier

Butterscotch Rolls

For your morning sweet tooth —

2 cups flour
4 teaspoons baking powder
2/3 teaspoon salt
4 tablespoons shortening
2/3 cup milk
3 tablespoons butter, creamed
1 cup brown sugar
1 cup nuts, chopped
Cinnamon and/or apricot jam (optional)

Preheat the oven to 375°F. Sift together the dry ingredients, add the shortening, and blend with a fork or pastry blender. Add the milk and stir to make a soft dough.

On a floured board, knead the dough slightly and roll out to a thickness of 1/8-inch. Spread the pastry with the creamed butter. Combine the brown sugar and nuts and sprinkle over the but-ter. Dust with the cinnamon and spread with jam if desired.

Roll up the pastry as if for a jelly roll, cut into 1-inch slices, and place seam side down on a buttered baking pan. Bake for 25–30 minutes, let cool slightly, and remove from the pan.
Yields 15–20

Dennis A. Nawrocki

Cadillac Mountain Blueberry Bread

An old and cherished recipe, this cakelike bread is best with a mixture of tart and sweet Michigan blueberries.

1 cup plus 4 tablespoons margarine or
        butter, softened
2 cups granulated sugar
4 eggs
2 teaspoons vanilla
2 teaspoons baking soda
4 tablespoons sour milk*
4 cups plus 4 tablespoons flour
1 teaspoon salt
4 teaspoons cinnamon
4 cups fresh blueberries
4 tablespoons brown sugar

Preheat the oven to 350°F. and grease 2 9- by 5-inch loaf pans. In a large bowl, cream together 1 cup of the margarine, the granulated sugar, eggs, and vanilla and set aside. Dissolve the baking soda in the sour milk and set aside. In a separate bowl, sift together 4 cups of the flour, the salt, and 2 teaspoons of the cin-namon and add to the butter and sugar mixture alternately with the sour milk mixture. Fold in the blueberries and pour the batter into the prepared loaf pans.

For the topping, combine the re-maining butter, flour, and cinnamon with the brown sugar and spread over the batter. Bake for 1 hour or until a cake tester inserted in the centers of the loaves comes out clean. Cool the loaves thor-oughly before slicing.

*If you do not have sour milk avail-able, combine approximately 1 teaspoon of vinegar or lemon juice with 1/4 cup of milk and let stand for 5 minutes or more before using.

Note: *Blueberry Bread* freezes well for up to several months.
Yields 2 loaves

Margaret Stensland

Jalapeño Cornbread

A spicy accompaniment for hearty Mexican chili —

1 cup cornmeal
1 cup flour
1 tablespoon baking powder
3/4 teaspoon salt
2 eggs, beaten lightly
1 cup milk
2 tablespoons bacon drippings

1 cup whole kernel corn
1 jalapeño pepper, chopped
3 tablespoons pimento, chopped

Preheat the oven to 350°F. and grease an 8-inch square pan. In a large bowl, com-bine all of the ingredients, mix well, and pour into the prepared pan. Bake for 35 minutes or until lightly browned. Let cool briefly before cutting into 9 equal squares.
Serves 5–9

The Cookbook Committee

Raphaelle Peale, American, 1774–1825, *Still Life with Wine Glass,* 1818, oil on panel, 26 x 34.6 cm. Founders Society Purchase, Laura H. Murphy Fund (39.7).

Honey Loaf Cake

This sweet yet spicy cake, traditionally served in September at the Jewish New Year, is now a favorite for any festive occasion.

5½ cups all-purpose flour
1½ teaspoons baking powder
1½ teaspoons baking soda
1 teaspoon allspice
1 teaspoon cloves
1 teaspoon nutmeg
1 teaspoon cinnamon
1 teaspoon ginger
4 eggs
2 cups sugar
1 pound honey
1¼ cups raisins
¾ cup vegetable oil
1 teaspoon vanilla extract
1 teaspoon lemon extract
1 teaspoon orange extract
1½ cups cold, strong coffee
½ cup sliced almonds

Preheat the oven to 325°F. Grease 2 loaf pans with vegetable oil and set aside. In a mixing bowl, sift together the flour, baking powder, baking soda, and spices and set aside.

In a large bowl, mix together the eggs, sugar, honey, raisins, vegetable oil, vanilla, lemon and orange extracts, and the coffee, blending until smooth. Gradually add the dry ingredients, mixing well after each addition.*

Pour the batter into the prepared pans, filling each approximately two-thirds full. Sprinkle the sliced almonds over the top of the loaves and bake for 80 minutes or until done. Remove from the oven and transfer to racks to cool.

*This step is best done by hand; a blender or food processor does not work well for this recipe.

Yields 2 loaves

Davira Taragin

Stone-ground Scones

Full-bodied nutty flavor —

½ cup stone-ground whole wheat flour
½ cup all-purpose flour
½ teaspoon cream of tartar
1 teaspoon baking soda
2–3 tablespoons sugar
¼ cup sweet butter, softened
⅓ cup plus 2 tablespoons light cream
½ cup golden raisins (optional)
Honey or raspberry jam (optional)

Preheat the oven to 400°F. and lightly grease a baking sheet. In a large bowl, combine the flour, cream of tartar, baking soda, and sugar and cut in the butter until the mixture resembles coarse meal. Stir in ⅓ cup of the cream and the raisins and pat the dough into a circular mound that measures approximately ½-inch thick at the edge and 2 inches thick in the center. Quarter the mound of dough, place the triangular pieces on the baking sheet, and brush the tops with the remaining 2 tablespoons cream. Bake for 15 minutes or until lightly browned. Serve warm with honey or raspberry jam.

   Yields 4

Elizabeth A. Ricker

Spirited Cornmeal Coffee Cake

Guaranteed to raise your spirits —

½ cup sugar
¼ cup butter
1 egg
½ cup plain yogurt
½ cup yellow cornmeal
1 cup all-purpose flour
1 teaspoon lemon peel, shredded finely
½ teaspoon baking soda
½ teaspoon salt
⅓ cup mixed fruits (such as dates, apricots, and raisins), chopped finely
Lemon-Rum Glaze (recipe follows)

Preheat the oven to 350°F. and grease and flour a 7½- by 3½-inch loaf pan. In a large bowl, cream together the sugar and butter and beat in the egg and yogurt. In a separate bowl, combine the cornmeal, flour, lemon peel, baking soda, and salt and stir slowly into the sugar and butter mixture. Add the chopped fruits, blend well, pour the batter into the prepared pan, and cover loosely with foil. Bake for 15 minutes, remove the foil, and continue to bake for an additional 45 minutes. Let the coffee cake cool for about 10 minutes in the pan, then remove from the pan and transfer to a wire rack. Pierce the top of the cake and pour *Lemon-Rum Glaze* across it while the cake is still warm. Cool the coffee cake completely, cover, and refrigerate overnight before serving.

   Serves 4

Lemon-Rum Glaze

¼ cup rum
2 tablespoons lemon juice
2 tablespoons sugar

In a small saucepan, combine all of the ingredients, place over medium heat, and stir until the sugar has dissolved completely. Use immediately.

   Yields ¼ cup

Natalie Lederer

Joseph Maria Olbrich, Austrian, 1867–1908, *Vase*, ca. 1900, glass and pewter, h. 24.8 cm. Founders Society Purchase, New Endowment Fund (F81.63).

Molasses Doughnuts

Also called "Yankee Cakes," doughnuts have become a favorite treat both North and South.

1 egg, beaten
½ cup sugar
1 cup molasses
½ cup buttermilk
2 tablespoons butter, melted
5 cups flour, sifted
1 tablespoon plus 2 teaspoons baking powder
¾ teaspoon baking soda
1 teaspoon salt
1 teaspoon nutmeg
1 teaspoon cinnamon
1 teaspoon ginger
Vegetable oil
2 teaspoons cinnamon combined with 1 cup sugar

In a large mixing bowl, combine the beaten egg and sugar, beat well, and stir in the molasses, buttermilk, and butter. In a separate bowl, sift together the flour, baking powder, baking soda, salt, and spices, add to the molasses mixture, and blend well. Cover the dough and place in the refrigerator to chill for 1 hour or more.

When chilled, divide the dough in half. Working with one portion at a time, place the dough on a floured board and roll to a thickness of ¼-inch. In a deep fryer, heat 3–4 inches of oil to 375°F. Cut only a few doughnuts at a time with a floured doughnut cutter, drop into the hot oil, and fry for 1 minute or until golden brown. Turn the doughnuts, fry the other sides briefly, remove, and drain on paper toweling. Repeat with the remaining dough. Roll the doughnuts in the cinnamon and sugar mixture before serving.

Yields 2½ dozen

Opal D. Suddeth-Hodge

South American Spice Bread

¡Olé!

2 packages dry yeast
¼ cup water, lukewarm
¼ teaspoon granulated sugar
⅓ cup plus 2 tablespoons butter, softened
¼ cup plus 2 tablespoons honey
¼ cup brown sugar
2 teaspoons salt
⅓ cup orange juice
2 cups milk, scalded
1 egg, beaten lightly
1 tablespoon cumin
4 cups whole wheat flour
3½ cups all-purpose flour

In a small pan, sprinkle the yeast over the lukewarm water, add the granulated sugar, and stir to dissolve. In a separate pan or bowl, add ⅓ cup of the butter, ¼ cup of the honey, the brown sugar, salt, and orange juice to the milk and let cool to lukewarm.

In a large bowl, combine the yeast mixture, egg, cumin, and whole wheat flour and beat until smooth. Mix in approximately 2½ cups of the all-purpose flour to make a stiff dough. Turn the dough onto a floured board and knead, using as much of the remaining flour as necessary to prevent sticking, until the dough is smooth and elastic. Place the dough in an oiled bowl, cover with a damp cloth, and set in a warm place to rise until doubled in bulk. Punch down the dough and knead for 1 minute before returning to the bowl and again letting it rise until doubled. Punch the dough down once more, shape into a ball, and divide into two pieces.

Preheat the oven to 425°F. and butter 2 9- by 5-inch loaf pans. Place the halves of dough in the prepared pans, cover, and let rise until doubled in bulk. Bake for 10 minutes, reduce the heat to 350°F., and continue to bake for 25–30 minutes or until the loaves sound hollow when tapped. Remove the loaves from the oven and place, still in the pans, on a wire rack to cool for about 5 minutes.

While the loaves are cooling, combine the remaining 2 tablespoons softened butter and the remaining honey. Remove the loaves from the pans and brush the butter and honey mixture across the tops. Let the loaves cool thoroughly before slicing.

Yields 2 loaves

Nancy Jones

DESSERTS AND COOKIES

No matter what the variety or proportions of a meal, satisfaction is not reached until dessert is served. Universally the favorite course of every meal, desserts, in the many ingenious forms we know them, are relative newcomers to the dining table.

Although sugar became a popular commodity in about 500 B.C., it was not until the early sixteenth century that sugar was for the first time combined with chocolate, and it was not until 1756 that the first factory devoted solely to the manufacture of chocolate confections was opened in Germany. The combination of sugar and chocolate has inspired a seemingly endless array of tempting concoctions. Not to be forgotten, however, are the fantastic creations featuring fruits, ice creams, nuts, and on and on to the delight of every sweet tooth. Following are a number of recipes guaranteed to end your meals with élan, although many could be considered as ends in themselves.

Good food, particularly a fine dessert at the end of a meal, and a relaxing atmosphere seem to stimulate deep conversation. Bistros and cafés have long been havens for friends to gather and discuss the latest developments in art, culture, politics, and sports. It is not surprising, then, that many artists have depicted such cafés with the same degrees of enthusiasm and lively energy that one would expect to experience in them. In *Café*, Ernst Ludwig Kirchner used large blocks of bold color to capture the charged atmosphere of a small café in which, doubtless, important discussions analyze the past and the direction of the future.

Ernst Ludwig Kirchner, German, 1880–1938, *Café* (detail), 1928, oil on canvas, 80 x 70 cm. Gift of Mr. and Mrs. A. D. Wilkinson (59.450).

Swedish Apple Pie

Luscious fruit and nuts without a "framing" crust —

1 egg
¾ cup sugar
1 teaspoon baking powder
¼ teaspoon salt
½ teaspoon cinnamon
¼ teaspoon vanilla extract
1 large Granny Smith apple, chopped
1 cup nuts, chopped
Whipped cream or Cinnamon Ice Cream
    (recipe follows)

Preheat the oven to 350°F. In a large mixing bowl, beat the egg until thick and lemon-colored, blend in the sugar, baking powder, salt, cinnamon, vanilla, apple, and nuts, and spoon into a greased 9-inch pie pan. Bake for 30 minutes, remove from the oven, and let cool slightly. Serve warm topped with whipped cream or *Cinnamon Ice Cream.*
    Serves 4–5

Cinnamon Ice Cream

1 quart vanilla ice cream
Cinnamon to taste

Slightly soften the ice cream, add cinnamon to taste, mix thoroughly, and refreeze.
    Yields 1 quart

Lucy Van Dusen

Baked Pears

Spirited still lifes —

4 Anjou or Bosc pears, peeled (leave stems
    attached)
4 teaspoons butter
2 tablespoons sugar
Juice of ½ lemon
½ teaspoon vanilla extract
2 tablespoons Drambuie, kirsch, or rum

Preheat the oven to 350°F. Cut a thin slice from the bottom of each pear so that it will stand upright. Place each pear in the center of a large square of aluminum foil and put 1 teaspoon of butter over each stem.
    Mix together the sugar, lemon juice, vanilla, and Drambuie, spoon the mixture equally over the pears, and pull up and seal the foil around them, covering completely. Place the pears in a baking dish,* bake for 1 hour, and let cool for 10 minutes before serving.
    The pears may be prepared in advance to this point.
    Serves 4

Nancy Heenan

Apple Torte

Delicate patterns of fruit topped by a rich custard-like sauce —

1 cup butter
2 cups sugar
4 eggs
1¾ cups flour
2 teaspoons baking powder
8–10 large apples, cored and quartered
    (or cut into eighths)
Cinnamon

In a saucepan, melt ½ cup of the butter, gradually beat in 1 cup of the sugar, and add 2 of the eggs, one at a time, blending thoroughly. Combine the flour and baking powder, add to the butter mixture, and beat well. Spread the dough over the bottom of a greased, 9-inch springform pan and cover completely with apple pieces, standing them on end to form a flower-like pattern. Sprinkle the torte with cinnamon and bake in a 350°F. oven for 1 hour.
    In the meantime, cream together the remaining butter and sugar and beat in the remaining eggs — the mixture should resemble a custard. Pour over the top of the baked torte, reduce the oven temperature to 300°F., and return to the oven to bake for 15 minutes or until the custard has set.
    Serves 6–8

Nettie Firestone

Mocha Mystery Cake

Its exquisite taste is no secret.

1 cup cake flour, sifted
1¼ cups granulated sugar
2 teaspoons baking powder
⅛ teaspoon salt
1 ounce chocolate
2 tablespoons butter
1 teaspoon vanilla extract
½ cup milk
½ cup brown sugar
4 tablespoons cocoa

1 cup strong coffee
Whipped cream

Preheat the oven to 350°F. In a large bowl, sift together the flour, ¾ cup of the granulated sugar, baking powder, and salt. Melt together the chocolate and butter and blend into the dry ingredients. Combine the vanilla and milk, add to the chocolate mixture, and blend thoroughly. Pour the batter into a greased, 8-inch square cake pan and set aside.

In a small bowl, combine the brown sugar, cocoa, and the remaining granulated sugar and sprinkle over the batter. Pour the coffee over all and bake for 40 minutes. Cut into squares and serve topped with whipped cream.

Serves 8

Norma Murray

Heirloom Fudge Cake

You'll want to add it to your treasury.

4 ounces unsweetened chocolate
1¼ cups hot water
2 cups sugar
2 cups flour
½ cup butter
3 eggs
5 teaspoons baking powder
2 teaspoons vanilla extract
Chocolate Mocha Buttercream Frosting
   (recipe follows)

Preheat the oven to 375°F. In the top of a double boiler, melt the chocolate, add the hot water, and stir to blend. In a bowl, cream together the sugar, flour, and butter, blend in the melted chocolate, and beat well. Cover and chill in the refrigerator for at least 1 hour.

After chilling, beat in the eggs, one at a time, add the baking powder and vanilla, and beat again. Pour the batter into a greased and floured 9- by 13-inch pan and bake for 10 minutes. Reduce the temperature to 275°F. and bake until done (approximately 45–50 minutes). Remove the cake from the oven, cool, and frost.

Serves 12

Chocolate Mocha Buttercream Frosting

3 tablespoons butter, softened
⅜ cup cocoa
1⅓ cups confectioner's sugar
¼ teaspoon lemon juice
½ teaspoon vanilla extract
2½ tablespoons hot, strong coffee

In a small bowl, cream together the butter, cocoa, confectioner's sugar, lemon juice, and vanilla. Add the coffee and beat until creamy.

Yields ¾–1 cup

Rema S. Frankel

Pots de Crème

Incredibly rich and smooth, yet simple —

2 cups heavy cream
¼ cup sugar
1⅓ cups chocolate chips
6 egg yolks, beaten
1 teaspoon vanilla extract
Whipped cream, sweetened and flavored
   with vanilla extract

In the top of a double boiler, combine the cream and sugar, scald lightly, remove from the heat, add the chocolate chips, and stir until completely blended. Add the beaten egg yolks to the chocolate mixture, return to the heat, and cook, stirring constantly, until the mixture has thickened. Remove from the heat and stir in the vanilla. Pour into *pots de crème* or custard cups, cool slightly, and refrigerate to chill. Serve topped with whipped cream.

Serves 6

Sarah Cinelli

Paul Revere II, American, 1735-1818, *Teapot,* ca. 1790-95, silver, h. 14.6 cm. Founders Society Purchase, Gibbs-Williams Fund (37.92).

Apple Fritters

Beer adds a very subtle flavor —

12 apples, peeled and cored
8 ounces flour
1½ cups beer
½ teaspoon salt
Oil for deep frying
Confectioner's sugar

Cut the apples crosswise into approximately ⅜-inch-thick slices and set aside. In a large bowl, combine the flour and beer, stir until smooth, and add the salt.

Heat the oil to about 375°F. Working quickly, dip the apple slices in the batter and fry until golden. Drain the fritters on paper towels and sprinkle with confectioner's sugar.
Yields 40-45

Tina Hills

Auntie Mar's Apricot Soufflé

The lightest froth of apricot —

1 cup dried apricots
Water
6 egg whites
¼ cup granulated sugar
Butter
Whipped cream (optional)
Shaved almonds, toasted (optional)
Liqueur Sauce
(recipe follows)

In a saucepan, combine the apricots with water to cover and boil gently for 15 minutes. Purée the mixture by putting through a food mill — it should be thick, not runny — and set aside.

Beat the egg whites, gradually adding the sugar as the whites begin to mound, until they are stiff but not dry. Fold in the apricot purée, stirring with a large fork or wire whisk.

Lightly butter and sprinkle with sugar the top half and lid of a 2½-quart double boiler. Transfer the soufflé mixture into the double boiler, cover, and cook over boiling water for 60 minutes. Gently remove the soufflé to a serving platter and garnish with a ring of whipped cream and toasted, shaved almonds. Serve with *Liqueur Sauce* on the side.

Note: To ensure the success of this soufflé, the water in the bottom of the double boiler must not boil away. The soufflé may be left to rest for approximately 40 minutes after cooking, but be sure to check the level of water and to keep the heat very low.
Serves 8

Liqueur Sauce

2 egg yolks
¼ cup sugar
½ pint heavy cream, whipped
2 tablespoons curaçao

Beat together the egg yolks and sugar, combine with the whipped cream, and stir in the curaçao just before serving.
Yields 1 cup

Nicole Stroh

Larry Devine's Carrot Cake

An eternal favorite —

2 cups flour
1 teaspoon salt
2 cups sugar
2 teaspoons baking powder
2 teaspoons baking soda
2 teaspoons cinnamon
Dash of nutmeg
4 eggs
1½ cups oil
3 cups carrots, grated
1 cup pecans, chopped
½ cup raisins
Cream Cheese Frosting
(recipe follows)

Preheat the oven to 300°F. In a large bowl, sift together the flour, salt, sugar, baking powder, baking soda, cinnamon, and nutmeg. Beat together the eggs and oil and combine with the dry ingredients. Fold in the carrots, pecans, and raisins, pour the batter into three greased, 9-inch cake pans, and bake for 45 minutes or until done. Let the layers cool slightly, remove from the pans, and transfer to a rack. Spread *Cream Cheese Frosting* between the layers and over the top and sides of the cake while it is still warm.
Serves 12

Cream Cheese Frosting

1 8-ounce package cream cheese, softened
8 ounces confectioner's sugar
½ cup butter, softened
1–2 teaspoons vanilla extract

Blend together the cream cheese, confectioner's sugar, butter, and vanilla and beat until smooth and creamy.
Yields approximately 2 cups

Margaret DeGrace

Apple and Honey Sundae

An elegant offering —

3 red apples, cored, quartered, and cut into pieces
4 tablespoons butter
3 tablespoons brown sugar
1 tablespoon cinnamon
2 tablespoons French brandy
1 scant cup honey (or to taste)

Vanilla ice cream
Nuts, chopped, or shredded coconut (optional)

In a 9-inch sauté pan, sauté the apple pieces in the butter for 1 minute. Add the brown sugar and cinnamon and cook for 1 minute more. Stir in the brandy, flame, and let the alcohol burn off. Add the honey, reheat, and stir to blend. Serve over vanilla ice cream with a garnish of chopped nuts and/or coconut.
Serves 6

Diane Schoenith

Summer Pudding

A sour-sweet fruit pudding —

1½ pounds rhubarb, cut into 1-inch pieces
¼ cup water
¼ cup sugar
20 ounces frozen, sweetened strawberries
1 loaf white bread, sliced (with crusts removed)
Whipping cream, sweetened and whipped lightly

In a large saucepan, combine the rhubarb, water, and sugar, cover, bring to a boil, and cook for approximately 5 minutes. Add the frozen strawberries, cook and stir until they are heated through, taste, and add more sugar if necessary.
Line a glass bowl with some of the bread, fill with the rhubarb and strawberry mixture, and cover with additional bread. Transfer to the refrigerator and chill overnight. Serve with sweetened, lightly whipped cream.
Note: Any combination of berries may be used for this pudding.
Serves 6

Eve Cockburn

Ukrainian Artist Cake

Now you, too, can create this work of art.

8 eggs
⅔ cup sugar
3 cups almonds, ground finely
Coffee Frosting or Chocolate Buttercream
    Frosting
    (recipes follow)
Pralin Powder
    (recipe follows)

Preheat the oven to 350°F. In a large bowl, beat the eggs with the sugar until almost stiff. Fold in the ground almonds a little at a time, stirring quickly but gently in one direction only. Pour the batter into a buttered, 10-inch spring-form pan and bake for 30 minutes or until a toothpick inserted in the center of the cake comes out clean.

When cool, use a serrated knife to halve the cake horizontally, spread *Coffee Frosting* between the layers, reassemble, and frost the top and sides with *Chocolate Buttercream Frosting*. Sprinkle with *Pralin Powder* and serve.

Serves 8–10

Coffee Frosting

8 ounces confectioner's sugar
    (approximately)
1 egg yolk
1 cup unsalted butter, softened
1 tablespoon strong coffee
1 teaspoon vanilla extract

In a mixing bowl, combine the confectioner's sugar, egg yolk, butter, coffee, and vanilla and blend thoroughly.

Yields approximately 2 cups

Chocolate Buttercream Frosting

4 egg yolks
¾ cup sugar
¾ cup water
Pinch of cream of tartar
1½ cups sweet butter, cut into small pieces
4 ounces semisweet chocolate
5 tablespoons strong, hot coffee
3 tablespoons rum

Using an electric mixer, beat the egg yolks until very light and set aside. In a saucepan, combine the sugar, water, and cream of tartar and cook until the mixture reaches the thread stage. Pour the syrup in a thin stream into the egg yolks, beating constantly, and add the butter.

Melt the chocolate in the coffee and add to the butter mixture along with the rum, beating thoroughly. Transfer to the refrigerator for 30 minutes to cool, remove, and beat until the frosting is light in color and no longer shiny.

Yields 1½–2 cups

Pralin Powder

½ cup sugar
½ cup slivered almonds

In a skillet, heat the sugar, stirring constantly, until it has melted and formed a light brown syrup. Stir in the almonds, pour onto a greased cookie sheet, and let stand to cool. Break into small pieces, place in a food processor, and process until ground to a fine powder.

Yields approximately ⅓ cup

Yuri Krochmaluk

Chocolate Mousse Cake

A chocolate lover's delight —

¾ cup unsalted butter
12 ounces semisweet chocolate
3 tablespoons instant coffee
2 tablespoons Scotch or brandy (optional)
9 extra-large eggs, separated
½ cup plus 1 tablespoon sugar
1½ cups heavy cream, whipped

Preheat the oven to 350°F. Grease a 9-inch springform pan, line with waxed paper, grease the paper, and set aside.

In the top of a double boiler, melt and stir together the butter, chocolate, and coffee, set aside to cool slightly, then stir in the Scotch or brandy. Beat the egg yolks until thick and lemon-colored, add the sugar, beat until light, and blend into the chocolate mixture. Beat the egg whites until stiff and fold gently into the chocolate mixture.

Pour one-half of the batter into the prepared pan, bake for 30 minutes, and set aside to cool. While the cake is baking, fold the whipped cream into the remaining batter, blend thoroughly, and refrigerate. When the cake has cooled sufficiently, pour the chilled batter over the top and place in the freezer. Approximately 20–30 minutes before serving, remove the frozen mousse cake from the freezer and decorate with shaved chocolate.

Serves 8–10

Lois Robinson

Chicago Boulevard Lemon Cake

Both tart and sweet, this dessert will make you want to do a cakewalk!

Fine, dry bread crumbs
3 cups all-purpose flour, sifted
2 teaspoons double-acting baking powder
½ teaspoon salt
1 cup butter
2¾ cups sugar
4 eggs
1 cup milk
Rind of 2 lemons, grated finely
Juice of 2 lemons

Preheat the oven to 350°F. Butter a 9- by 3½-inch tube pan and dust lightly with fine bread crumbs. Sift together the flour, baking powder, and salt and set aside.

Cream together the butter and 2 cups of the sugar, beat for 2–3 minutes, then beat in the eggs one at a time. Slowly add the dry ingredients alternately with the milk, blending thoroughly after each addition. Stir in the lemon rind and pour into the prepared pan. Bake for 70–85 minutes or until a toothpick or cake tester inserted in the center of the cake comes out clean. Let the cake stand for approximately 3 minutes, invert, and remove from the pan.

Combine the lemon juice and remaining sugar, stir until the sugar has dissolved, and brush over the hot cake — the glaze should be absorbed completely. Let cool for at least 2 hours before serving.

Serves 10–12

Dorothy Karpus

Fresh Apple Cake

An old-fashioned treat —

1½ cups corn oil
1½–2 cups sugar
3 large eggs
3 cups flour, sifted
2 teaspoons vanilla extract
2 teaspoons baking soda
¾ teaspoon salt
1 teaspoon cinnamon
3 cups apples, chopped
1 cup nuts, chopped
Brown Sugar Glaze
    (recipe follows)

Preheat the oven to 350°F. In a large bowl, combine the oil, sugar, eggs, flour, vanilla, baking soda, salt, and cinnamon and blend thoroughly. Fold in the apples and nuts and pour into a greased 9- by 13-inch pan. Bake for 35 minutes, remove from the oven, prick the cake with a fork, and cover with glaze while still warm. Serve immediately.

Serves 15–20

Brown Sugar Glaze

½ cup butter
1 cup light brown sugar
½ cup evaporated milk
1 teaspoon vanilla extract

In a saucepan, combine the butter, brown sugar, and evaporated milk. Bring to a boil, cook for 2½ minutes, add the vanilla, and stir to blend.

Yields approximately 1 cup

Dorothy Roper

Strawberry Ice Cream

Succulent berries captured in cream yield old-fashioned flavor.

1 16-ounce package frozen strawberries,
    thawed slightly
1 pint sour cream
½ cup sugar
1 tablespoon lemon juice
Fresh strawberries, rinsed, drained, and
    dipped in chocolate (optional)

In a large bowl, combine the strawberries, sour cream, sugar, and lemon juice, blend thoroughly, and pour into ice trays. Place in the freezer for about 45 minutes, remove, and beat with a fork or whisk. Pour the mixture into a 1½- to 2-quart mold and re-freeze for 2 hours or more. Unmold the ice cream onto a serving platter and surround with fresh, chocolate-tipped strawberries.

Serves 6

Virginia McMillan

Chocolate Pecan Pie

Sublime beyond imagination!

2 ounces unsweetened chocolate
3 tablespoons butter
1 cup light corn syrup
3/4 cup sugar
3 eggs, beaten lightly
1 teaspoon vanilla extract
1 cup pecans, chopped coarsely
1 9-inch unbaked pie crust
Whipped cream

Preheat the oven to 375°F. In the top of a double boiler, melt the chocolate and the butter and stir to blend. In a saucepan, combine the corn syrup and sugar, bring to a boil, and cook for 2 minutes. Blend together the chocolate and syrup mixtures and pour slowly over the beaten eggs, stirring constantly. Add the vanilla and pecans, pour the batter into the un-baked crust, and bake for 45–50 minutes or until the top of the pie has puffed up. Remove from the oven, cool, and serve while still warm topped with whipped cream.

Serves 8

Elsie H. Peck

Frozen Grand Marnier Soufflé with Hot Strawberry Sauce

The triumphant finale to a formal meal —

1 pint vanilla ice cream, softened slightly
2 macaroons, crumbled
4 teaspoons Grand Marnier
1/2 cup heavy cream
1--2 tablespoons almonds, toasted and
    chopped
1–2 teaspoons confectioner's sugar
Hot Strawberry Sauce
    (recipe follows)

In a large bowl, thoroughly blend the softened ice cream, macaroons, and Grand Marnier. Whip the cream until thick and shiny, fold into the ice cream mixture, and spoon into a 3-cup metal serving dish or mold. Sprinkle the surface lightly with toasted almonds and confectioner's sugar, cover with plastic wrap, and freeze until firm (about 4–5 hours).

When ready to serve, unmold onto a chilled platter, cut into slices, and top with *Hot Strawberry Sauce.*

Serves 4

Hot Strawberry Sauce

1 pint fresh strawberries, rinsed, hulled,
    and halved (or 1 10-ounce package of
    frozen, sliced strawberries, thawed)
1/4 cup sugar (or to taste; less sugar is
    necessary with frozen berries)
4 teaspoons orange juice or Grand
    Marnier

In a saucepan, combine the berries and sugar, stir to blend, and simmer until soft but not mushy. Remove the pan from the heat and stir in the orange juice or Grand Marnier.

Yields 1½–2 cups

Barbara G. Fleischman

Frozen Lemon Mousse

Cool and tangy — a summer sensation!

Graham cracker crumbs
1 8-ounce can sweetened condensed milk
1 6-ounce can frozen lemonade concentrate,
    thawed
1 teaspoon lemon juice
1 pint whipping cream, whipped to form
    stiff peaks
Fresh berries or orange sections (optional)

Spread a thin layer of graham cracker crumbs in the bottom of a 9-inch square cake pan and set aside.

In a large bowl, combine the condensed milk, thawed lemonade concentrate, and lemon juice and fold in the whipped cream, blending thoroughly. Pour over the graham cracker crumbs, sprinkle lightly with additional graham cracker crumbs, cover with plastic wrap, and freeze.

To serve, cut into squares and top with fresh berries or orange sections.

Serves 9

The Cookbook Committee

Charles Demuth, American, 1833–1935, *Still Life: Apples and Bananas,* 1925, watercolor over pencil, 30.2 x 45.7 cm. Bequest of Robert H. Tannahill (70.253).

Brandied Caramel Flan

Especially appropriate for menus with a Spanish theme —

1¼ cups sugar
2 cups milk
2 cups light cream
6 eggs, beaten
½ teaspoon salt
2 teaspoons vanilla extract
⅓ cup brandy
Boiling water

Preheat the oven to 325°F. In a large saucepan, cook ¾ cup of the sugar over medium heat until it has melted and formed a light brown syrup. Stir the syrup until it is of a uniform consistency and pour into a heated, shallow, 8½-inch round baking dish. Rotate the dish quickly so that the syrup completely covers the bottom and sides and set aside.

In a medium saucepan, heat the milk and cream until bubbles form around the edge of the pan, set aside, and keep warm. To the beaten eggs, add the salt, vanilla, and remaining sugar, gradually stir in the hot milk mixture and the brandy, and pour into the syrup-coated baking dish. Set the dish in a shallow pan, surround with boiling water to a depth of ½-inch, and bake for 35–40 minutes or until a silver knife inserted in the custard comes out clean. Let stand to cool, then refrigerate for 4 hours or overnight.

To serve, run a small spatula around the edge of the dish to loosen the flan, invert over a shallow serving dish, and shake gently to release.

Serves 8

Diane Denaro Frank

Florentine Trifle

Like a fine work of art —

1 pound cake or spongecake
Ladyfingers
2–3 tablespoons Madeira or sherry
Walnuts or pecans, chopped
2 cups vanilla custard or pudding mix
2 cups chocolate custard or pudding mix
1–2 tablespoons brandy (or medium or dark rum)
1 tablespoon confectioner's sugar
½ pint whipping cream

Cut the cake into ½-inch slices and line the bottom of a crystal bowl. Line the sides of the bowl with ladyfingers placed on end. Sprinkle the cake with a little Madeira or sherry, cover with a layer of chopped nuts, and cover the nuts with a layer of vanilla custard. Repeat the layers using the chocolate custard, then the vanilla again, and so on until the bowl is almost full. Refrigerate for several hours or until chilled through.

Gradually add the brandy and the confectioner's sugar to the whipping cream and whip until stiff peaks form. Use a spoon or pastry tube to decorate the top of the trifle, covering it completely with the whipped cream.

Serves 8

Florence Maiullo Barnes

Pumpkin Pudding

Light and airy — like a pumpkin pie without the crust.

3 eggs, separated
1 cup milk
2 cups canned pumpkin
1 teaspoon ginger
½ teaspoon cinnamon
¾ cup sugar
½ teaspoon salt
½ cup nuts, chopped
2 tablespoons brandy
Ice cream or whipped cream (optional)

Preheat the oven to 350°F. In a mixing bowl, beat together the egg yolks and milk, add the pumpkin, spices, and sugar, and blend thoroughly. In a separate bowl, beat the egg whites until stiff peaks form, fold into the pumpkin mixture, add the salt, nuts, and brandy, and stir to blend.

Pour the pudding into a buttered medium casserole or soufflé dish, place in a shallow pan of hot water, and bake for 1 hour or until a knife inserted in the center of the pudding comes out clean. Serve warm with ice cream or whipped cream.

Serves 6–8

Natalie Lederer

Ice Cream Cake

Extraordinary — and almost effortless!

1 dozen ladyfingers
Brownies
    (recipe follows)
1 10-ounce jar hot fudge topping
1 quart chocolate swirl ice cream, softened
1 quart coffee ice cream, softened
½ pint heavy cream, whipped

Line the sides of a 9-inch springform pan with ladyfingers. Crumble the brownies, spread one-half of them over the bottom of the pan, and cover with one-half of the hot fudge topping. Spread 1 quart of the ice cream over the topping, repeat the layers of brownies and fudge, and top with the remaining ice cream. Cover the pan with foil and place in the freezer until firm. Remove from the freezer approximately 20 minutes before serving and top with whipped cream.

> Serves 12–16

Brownies

1 cup butter
2 cups sugar
4 eggs
1 teaspoon vanilla extract
4 ounces unsweetened chocolate, melted
1 cup flour
2 cups walnuts, chopped
½ teaspoon salt

Preheat the oven to 350°F. Cream together the butter and sugar, beat in the eggs one at a time, and add the remaining ingredients. Bake in a well-greased 9- by 12-inch pan for 20–25 minutes — the brownies should be a little underdone — and let cool in the pan.

> Yields 12–16

Carole Frank

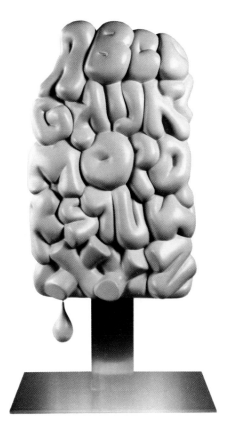

Claes Oldenburg, American, b. 1929, *Alphabet/Good Humor*, 1975, painted fiberglass and bronze, 91.4 x 40.6 x 17.8 cm. Founders Society Purchase, with donations from W. Hawkins Ferry (77.14).

Chocolate Danish Velvet

Sinfully smooth and rich —

Butter Crunch Crust or Topping
    (recipe follows)
1 8-ounce package cream cheese
½ cup sugar
1½ teaspoons vanilla extract
2 egg yolks, beaten
6 ounces semisweet chocolate, melted
2 egg whites
1 cup whipped cream
¾ cup pecans, chopped

Reserve ¾ cup of the freshly baked *Butter Crunch* crumbs for topping, press the remaining crumbs into the bottom of a 9-inch round cake pan, and set aside to cool.

Cream together the cream cheese, ¼ cup of the sugar, and the vanilla and stir in the egg yolks and the melted chocolate. Beat the egg whites, gradually adding the remaining sugar, and fold into the chocolate mixture. Fold in the whipped cream and pecans. Pour the batter over the crumb crust, sprinkle with the reserved topping, and freeze until firm.

> Serves 9–12

Butter Crunch Crust or Topping

½ cup butter
¼ cup brown sugar
1 cup flour
½ cup nuts

Preheat the oven to 400°F. Thoroughly combine the ingredients and spread in a 13- by 9-inch dish. Bake for 15 minutes and stir to break up into crumbs.

> Yields 1½–2 cups

Marge Seiger

Marquise Fondant au Coulis de Framboises

This chocolate mousse with raspberry sauce was served at the 1983 fundraiser "Under the Stars IV"; compliments are still echoing in the museum's halls!

1 cup whipping cream
1 pound bitter or semisweet chocolate,
    broken into small pieces
¼ cup unsalted butter
⅓ cup strong coffee, room temperature
2 large egg yolks
⅓ cup Kahlua
4 large egg whites, room temperature
4 tablespoons sugar
Tuiles, molded into an open shell shape (see
    recipe p. 153)
Raspberry Sauce
    (recipe follows)
Pralin Powder
    (optional; see recipe p. 140)

Beat the cream until stiff peaks form and set aside. In the top of a double boiler, melt the chocolate with the butter and coffee. In a small bowl, combine the egg yolks and the Kahlua and whisk into the chocolate mixture. Beat the egg whites until soft peaks form, gradually add the sugar, and continue to beat until the peaks become stiff. Fold the egg whites into the chocolate mixture, fold in the whipping cream, and pour into a shallow bowl. Cover and chill for approximately 6 hours.

Place the tuiles on individual plates, top with a large spoonful of the chocolate "mousse," drizzle with *Raspberry Sauce*, and sprinkle with *Pralin Powder*.
    Serves 8

Raspberry Sauce

1 pint frozen raspberries, thawed
Sugar to taste

Purée the raspberries in a food processor and put through a fine strainer to remove the seeds. Taste, add sugar if desired, and stir to blend.
    Yields approximately 1 cup

The Cookbook Committee

Persimmon Pudding with Lemon Sauce

This fall treat tastes even better the second day.

3–4 ripe persimmons (approximately
    1 quart), left unpeeled
3 eggs
1¼ cups sugar
1½ cups flour
1 teaspoon baking powder
1 teaspoon baking soda
½ teaspoon salt
½ cup butter, melted
½ cup milk or half-and-half
2 teaspoons cinnamon
1 teaspoon ginger
½ teaspoon freshly grated nutmeg
1 cup raisins (optional)
Nuts, chopped (optional)
Lemon Sauce
    (recipe follows)

Preheat the oven to 325°F. With scissors, cut the persimmons into 1-inch pieces. In a large bowl, combine the persimmon pieces and the remaining ingredients (except for the sauce) and beat thoroughly. Pour the mixture into a greased 2-quart casserole or 9-inch square baking dish, place the dish in a shallow pan of water, and bake for 2 hours or until the pudding is firm.* Serve warm with *Lemon Sauce*.

*The pudding batter may also be divided between two 1-quart casseroles and baked for 1–1½ hours. Enjoy one pudding fresh from the oven and freeze the other.
    Serves 8

Lemon Sauce

1 cup sugar
2 tablespoons cornstarch
2 cups water
Rind of 1 lemon, grated
4 tablespoons butter
3 tablespoons lemon juice
¼ teaspoon salt

In a saucepan over low heat, combine the sugar, cornstarch, water, and lemon rind and cook, stirring constantly, until the mixture has thickened. Add the butter, lemon juice, and salt and stir until smooth.
    Yields approximately 2 cups

Phyllis C. McLean

Frozen Chocolate Rum Bombe

A marvelous mold of fruit and chocolate —

½ cup fresh pineapple, cubed
½ cup candied cherries, halved
½ cup candied fruit mixture, diced
Rum
1 cup whipping cream
¼ cup confectioner's sugar
½ cup pecans, chopped
1 quart chocolate ice cream (or 1 quart
    strawberry water ice), softened slightly

In a large pan or bowl, cover the fruit in rum and soak overnight. Beat the cream until stiff peaks form and add the confectioner's sugar, the fruit and rum, and the nuts. Line a 2-quart melon mold with the ice cream or water ice and fill with the whipped cream and fruit mixture. Place in the freezer for at least 4 hours or overnight. Unmold carefully and serve immediately.

Serves 8

Marguerite Stroh

Chinese, *Tea Pot with Cover,* Yüan Dynasty, Lung-ch'üan celadon ware, h. with cover 8.3 cm. Gift of the Honorable and Mrs. G. Mennen Williams (72.672).

Apple Dumplings

Melt-in-your-mouth scrumptious!

1 cup granulated sugar
4–5 tablespoons cinnamon
2 cups flour
3 teaspoons baking powder
¼ teaspoon salt
⅓ cup shortening
½ cup milk
6 medium apples, peeled and cored
1 cup brown sugar
½ cup butter
2 cups water

Preheat the oven to 375°F. In a small bowl, combine ¾ cup of the granulated sugar and the cinnamon, stir to blend, and set aside.

In a separate bowl, combine the flour, baking powder, salt, and remaining granulated sugar, blend in the shortening and milk, and divide the dough into six portions.

On a floured board, roll each portion into an 8- or 9-inch circle and place an apple in the center. Add 2 tablespoons of the sugar and cinnamon mixture, wrap the dough around the apple, and press the edges firmly to seal. Arrange the dumplings in a baking dish.

In a small saucepan, combine the brown sugar, butter, and water, bring to a boil, and stir until the sugar has dissolved. Cover the dumplings with the brown sugar sauce, bake for 30 minutes, reduce the heat to 325°F., and bake an additional 30 minutes or until the apples are tender.

Serves 6

Winnie Polk

Soufflé-top Lemon Pudding

The dessert solution for suppers en famille —

2¼ cups sugar
5 tablespoons flour
¼ teaspoon salt
5 tablespoons butter
6 eggs, separated
2 cups milk
¾ cup lemon juice
Rind of 3 lemons, grated

Preheat the oven to 325°F. In a large bowl, sift together the sugar, flour, and salt, add the butter, and blend thoroughly. In a separate bowl, lightly beat the egg yolks, stir in the milk, and add to the butter mixture. Blend in the lemon juice and grated rind. Beat the egg whites until stiff peaks form, fold into the lemon mixture, and pour into a lightly buttered 2-quart baking dish. Set the dish in a shallow pan of hot water and bake for 50 minutes. Serve warm or chilled.

Serves 6–8

Mrs. John Booth

Boccone Dolce

"Sweet mouthful" is definitely an understatement when referring to this sinfully rich dessert!

4 egg whites
Pinch of salt
¼ teaspoon cream of tartar
1 cup plus 2 tablespoons sugar
6 ounces semisweet chocolate
3 tablespoons water
3 cups heavy cream
1 pint fresh strawberries, sliced

Preheat the oven to 250°F. In a large bowl, combine the egg whites, salt, and cream of tartar and beat until stiff but not dry. Gradually beat in 1 cup of the sugar until the whites become glossy.

Spread the meringue about ¼-inch thick in three 8-inch circles on a non-stick baking sheet. Bake for 20–25 minutes or until the meringues just begin to color but are still pliable. Remove the meringues from the oven, transfer to racks, and let cool.

In the top of a double boiler, combine the chocolate and water, stir until the chocolate has melted completely, and set aside to cool. Whip the cream until stiff peaks form and, while still beating, gradually add the remaining 2 tablespoons sugar — the whipped cream should become very stiff and glossy. Spread a thin coating of the cooled chocolate over the meringues, cover with a ¾-inch-thick layer of whipped cream, and top with a layer of sliced strawberries. Repeat the layers once more and add a final meringue on top. Frost the sides completely with whipped cream, decorate with additional strawberries, and/or drizzle with the remaining chocolate. Refrigerate for at least 2 hours before serving.

Serves 8

Trudi Wineman

Teahouse Cookies

Delicate and delicious —

1 cup butter, softened
1 cup sugar (plus sugar for coating)
1 egg
1 teaspoon vanilla extract
2⅓ cups flour

Preheat the oven to 350°F. In a mixing bowl, cream together the butter and 1 cup sugar, beat in the egg and vanilla, and blend in the flour. Shape the dough into small balls, roll in sugar (coating thoroughly), and place on ungreased cookie sheets. Flatten the cookies with the tines of a fork or the buttered bottom of a glass. Bake for 8–10 minutes, remove from the cookie sheets immediately, and cool on racks.

Note: These cookies freeze very well.
Yields 6–8 dozen

Jane Manoogian

Hawaiian Wedding Cake

A tropical delight —

2 cups sugar
2 cups flour
2 eggs
1 teaspoon baking soda
1 20-ounce can crushed pineapple (with liquid)
Wedding Veil Frosting
    (recipe follows)

Preheat the oven to 350°F. In a large bowl blend together the sugar, flour, eggs, baking soda, and pineapple and pour into a greased and floured 9- by 12-inch pan. Bake for 50 minutes or until a toothpick inserted in the center of the cake comes out clean. Frost the cake while it is still warm and serve.

Serves 16

Wedding Veil Frosting

1 3-ounce package cream cheese, softened
1 cup confectioner's sugar
1 teaspoon vanilla extract
¼ cup butter or margarine, softened

In a small bowl, combine the cream cheese, confectioner's sugar, vanilla, and butter and blend until completely smooth.

Yields approximately 1 cup

Bruce and Florence McVety

Jean-Honoré Fragonard, French, 1732–
1806, *The Grape Gatherer* (detail) from
Scenes of Country Life, 1753, oil on canvas,
143.5 x 90.2 cm. Founders Society Purchase,
Mr. and Mrs. Horace E. Dodge Memorial
Fund (71.391).

Lemon Cream Wafers with Strawberry Sauce

Delicate and delectable —

2¼ cups unsalted butter, cut into pieces
2 cups confectioner's sugar, sifted
½ teaspoon vanilla extract
2 egg yolks
3 cups all-purpose flour, sifted
Lemon Cream
    (recipe follows)
Strawberry Sauce
    (recipe follows)
20–25 fresh strawberries, rinsed

Preheat the oven to 400°F. In a large bowl, cream the butter until fluffy, add the confectioner's sugar, and beat well. Add the vanilla, beat, and add the egg yolks one at a time, beating after each addition. Thoroughly blend in the flour (if the dough is sticky add 1 tablespoon additional flour), roll the dough into a ball, wrap in waxed paper, and chill for 1–2 hours or until firm (do not chill overnight or the dough will become too hard to roll). Using a pastry cloth, roll out the dough to a thickness of ¼-inch and cut into 4-inch circles. Bake on ungreased cookie sheets for 6–10 minutes or until the edges begin to turn golden brown (watch closely because the wafers burn easily). Remove from the oven and let stand for 1 minute before transferring to a rack.* When cool, cover with the *Lemon Cream*, place on individual plates, surround with *Strawberry Sauce*, and decorate with a whole strawberry placed in the center of each wafer.

*The wafers may be made in advance and frozen.
    Yields 20–25

Lemon Cream

Zest of 4 lemons, chopped finely
Juice of 4 lemons
1 cup unsalted butter, cut into pieces
2 cups sugar
4 eggs, beaten lightly

In a large saucepan, combine all of the ingredients and bring just to a boil, stirring constantly. Remove from the heat, put through a fine strainer to remove the lemon zest, and place in the refrigerator to chill overnight. Stir to blend before using.
    Yields approximately 4 cups

Strawberry Sauce

2 quarts fresh strawberries, rinsed and
    hulled (or equivalent of frozen
    strawberries, thawed)
Sugar to taste (optional)

Purée the strawberries in a food processor and put through a fine strainer to remove the seeds. Taste and add sugar if desired.*
    *The sauce may be made in advance and refrigerated until needed.
    Yields 2 cups

Elizabeth May

Mousse Brillat-Savarin

A white chocolate mousse with fresh strawberries —

¾ cup sugar
¼ teaspoon cream of tartar
⅓ cup water
Pinch of salt
4 egg whites
12 ounces white chocolate, chopped finely
5 tablespoons kirsch
2 cups heavy cream
2–3 quarts fresh strawberries, rinsed and
    hulled

In a 1- to 1½-quart saucepan, combine the sugar, cream of tartar, and water and cook over moderate heat, stirring constantly, until the sugar has dissolved and the mixture comes to a boil. Dip a pastry brush in water and wash down the sides of the pan to remove any undissolved sugar granules. Insert a candy thermometer, increase the heat to high, and let boil (without stirring) until the syrup reaches the soft ball stage (between 234–240°F.).

Add the salt to the egg whites and beat until stiff but not dry. While beating at high speed, add the syrup in a thin stream to the egg whites and continue to beat for 3 minutes or until the mixture becomes very thick. Fold in the white chocolate — if the mixture is still warm, let stand until room temperature.

In a small bowl, add 2 tablespoons of the kirsch to the cream and whip until soft peaks form. Fold into the cooled chocolate mixture, pour into a large serving bowl, cover, and freeze.

In a separate bowl, combine the strawberries, sugar (if necessary), and the remaining kirsch. Remove the mousse from the freezer, spoon out onto individual serving plates, and garnish with the strawberries.
    Serves 10–12

Lee Frank

Japanese, *Vessel for Hot Water (Yutō)*, Muromachi Period, late 15th/early 16th cent., lacquer, negoro ware of red lacquer over black with zelkova wood band, h. 32 x diam. 24.3 cm. Founders Society Purchase, Acquisitions Fund (1983.1).

Scottish Banbury Tarts

Try them at teatime —

½ *cup butter, softened, plus 3 tablespoons butter, melted*
1 3-ounce package cream cheese, softened
1 cup flour, sifted
⅛ *teaspoon salt*
½ *cup currants*
Boiling water
2 eggs
1 cup brown sugar
½ *cup walnuts or pecans, chopped*

In a large bowl, cream together the softened butter and the cream cheese, add the flour and salt, and blend thoroughly. Form the dough into a ball, cover in plastic wrap, and chill for 1 hour or more.

Working with one-half of the dough at a time (keep the remaining dough refrigerated), roll out on a well-floured surface and cut with a 1½- to 2-inch round cutter. Line miniature tart pans with the rounds of dough, pressing into place to form small cups.

Preheat the oven to 425°F. Soak the currants in boiling water for 15 minutes and drain well. In a large bowl, cream together the eggs and brown sugar, add the nuts and melted butter, and fold in the currants. Fill the unbaked tart shells, place in the oven, and reduce the heat to 300°F. Bake for 15–20 minutes or until the crusts turn golden.

Yields 24–30

Carolyn Lundberg

Tarte aux Raisins

This grape flan adds a flair to any meal.

2 teaspoons cinnamon
1½ cups plus 2 tablespoons flour, separated
¾ *cup plus 6 tablespoons sugar*
Pinch of salt
6 tablespoons unsalted butter, softened
3 tablespoons vegetable oil
2 tablespoons hot water
1 egg
2 egg yolks
1 cup pineapple juice
2 cups white grapes, stemmed
Few drops of water

Preheat the oven to 425°F. Butter a 9- or 10-inch tart pan that has a removable bottom and set aside.

Sprinkle the cinnamon over 1½ cups of the flour, add the 6 tablespoons sugar and the salt, and mix thoroughly. Make a well in the center of the dry ingredients and blend in the butter and oil. Add the hot water, stir to blend, form the dough into a ball, and place in the prepared tart pan.

Using the palm of your hand, spread the dough to cover the tart pan, taking care to press the dough thinner at the base of the sides of the shell. Press a sheet of waxed paper or kitchen parchment over the pastry and weight with raw rice or dried beans. Bake for 15 minutes, remove the weights and paper, and bake an additional 5 minutes or until done. Transfer the shell to the refrigerator to chill.

To prepare the filling, combine the egg and egg yolks with ¼ cup of the sugar in a 2½-quart stainless steel or enameled saucepan. Beat with a whisk until light and lemon-colored, add the remaining 2 tablespoons flour, and beat until smooth. Whisk in the pineapple juice, place over low heat, and stir until the mixture comes to a boil. Cook for 2 minutes, stirring constantly, remove from the heat, and transfer to the refrigerator to chill.

Approximately 1 hour before serving, spread the cream filling in the tart shell and arrange the grapes over the top. In a small saucepan, combine the remaining sugar with a few drops of water, cook until the sugar has caramelized, and drizzle over the grapes. Serve immediately.

Note: This flan may be made with any combination of tart-flavored fruits such as plums or kiwis.

Serves 8

Edna Skinner

Crème Brulée

A feat of French cuisine —

1 quart heavy cream
2 tablespoons sugar
8 egg yolks, beaten well
1 teaspoon vanilla extract
¾–1 cup light brown sugar

Preheat the oven to 350°F. In the top of a double boiler, combine the cream and sugar, stir until the sugar has dissolved and the mixture is hot, and pour over the egg yolks. Add the vanilla, blending thoroughly, and pour the batter into a 9- by 2-inch round baking dish. Set the dish in a larger pan and surround with hot water to a depth of about 1 inch. Bake for 1 hour, let stand to cool, and refrigerate overnight.

Remove the custard from the refrigerator and cover the top with ¼-inch of finely sifted light brown sugar. Place the custard under the broiler approximately 4–6 inches from the flame. Leaving the oven door open, watch carefully until the sugar has melted, remove the custard, and return to the refrigerator to chill (the sugar will harden into a glaze).

Serves 6

Ann Katz

Irish Lace Cookies

Lovely to behold, and luscious as well —

¾ cup brown sugar, packed firmly
½ cup butter, softened
2 tablespoons flour
2 tablespoons milk
1 teaspoon vanilla extract
1¼ cups old-fashioned rolled oats

Preheat the oven to 350°F. Cream together the brown sugar and butter, beat in the flour, milk, and vanilla, and stir in the rolled oats. Drop the dough by slightly rounded teaspoonfuls approximately 2 inches apart onto a lightly greased cookie sheet. Bake for 6–9 minutes or until golden brown. Remove from the oven and let stand for 1 minute before loosening the cookies and transferring to a rack.

Yields 3 dozen

Trudi Wineman

Truffles

Heaven on earth —

1 cup butter
½ teaspoon vanilla extract
1 cup confectioner's sugar
2 cups flour, sifted
8 ounces sweet chocolate, ground finely
8 ounces almonds (approximately 1⅔ cups), ground finely
2 egg whites, beaten until stiff but not dry

Using an electric mixer, cream the butter in a large bowl, add the vanilla and confectioner's sugar, and mix until well blended and smooth. Add the flour and beat on low speed, scraping the bowl with a rubber spatula, until the mixture holds together. Transfer the pastry dough to a piece of waxed paper, flatten slightly, and shape into an oblong. Wrap the dough tightly and refrigerate while preparing the filling.

Preheat the oven to 375°F. In a food processor or bowl, combine the chocolate and almonds, fold in the beaten egg whites, and blend just until the mixture holds together. Divide the chocolate mixture into 60 pieces of approximately ¾ teaspoon each, shape into small balls, and place on waxed paper.

Remove the pastry from the refrigerator and cut into 60 small squares. Working with one piece of dough at a time, flatten the pastry in the palm of your hand and wrap around the chocolate filling, taking care to cover the chocolate completely. Roll the truffle into a ball, dusting hands with confectioner's sugar if the dough begins to stick. Place the truffles on an ungreased baking sheet about 1 inch apart and bake in the top one-third of the oven for 18–20 minutes or until very lightly browned.

Yields 60

Dee Dee Feldman

French Tuiles

The best tea trays are topped with these delicate French "tiles."

6 egg whites
1²⁄₃ cups sugar
¼ teaspoon salt
1 cup butter, melted and cooled slightly
1 cup flour, sifted
¾ cup blanched almonds, chopped finely

Preheat the oven to 350°F. Combine the egg whites, sugar, and salt and beat until the sugar is completely incorporated into the whites — they should be thick but not stiff. Gradually add the butter, fold in the flour and almonds, blend well, and drop by tablespoonfuls about 3 inches apart onto a cookie sheet that has been lined with parchment paper. Bake for 8–10 minutes.

Working quickly, remove one cookie at a time from the cookie sheet, place face down on a covered board or counter, and roll loosely around the handle of a wooden spoon to form a tube. Immediately slide the cookie off the handle and place on a rack to cool. If the cookies begin to cool and harden before they are rolled, return them to the oven briefly and continue.

Yields approximately 2½ dozen

Ruth Glancy

Polish Butter Cookies

Dress up these creations with nut and seed toppings.

1 cup butter
¾ cup sugar
5 hard-boiled egg yolks, sieved
1 teaspoon vanilla extract
2 cups flour, sifted
½ teaspoon salt
1 egg combined with 1 teaspoon milk
Nuts, chopped finely (optional)

Poppy seeds (optional)
½ teaspoon cinnamon combined with
       2²⁄₃ tablespoons sugar (optional)

Preheat the oven to 350°F. Cream together the butter and sugar, stir in the egg yolks, vanilla, flour, and salt, blend thoroughly, and place in the refrigerator to chill.

On a floured cloth, roll the dough to a thickness of ¼-inch, cut into shapes with cutters, and place the cookies on greased cookie sheets. Brush the tops of the cookies with the egg and milk mixture, top with nuts, poppy seeds, or cinnamon and sugar, and bake for 12 minutes or until lightly browned.

Yields 4 dozen

Judith Weston

Social Butterflies

Made with a rosette iron, these cookies are fast and easy, light and airy.

1½ cups flour, sifted
1 15-ounce can evaporated milk
¾ cup water
1½ teaspoons granulated sugar
½ teaspoon salt
2 eggs
Vegetable shortening
Confectioner's sugar

In a large bowl, combine the flour, evaporated milk, water, granulated sugar, salt, and eggs, blend thoroughly, and chill for 1 hour or more. Let the butter stand until room temperature.

Half fill a 1-quart saucepan or wok with vegetable shortening and heat to 350°F. Dip the rosette iron into the hot shortening, dip quickly into the batter (being careful that the batter does not come up over the edge of the iron), and dip in the hot shortening again — the rosette should fall away from the iron and float until golden brown. Remove, drain on paper towels, and sprinkle with confectioner's sugar while still warm. The rosettes are best served immediately but may be stored temporarily in a brown paper bag.

Yields 3–4 dozen

Alice Hoffer

Nighty-Nights

The ultimate bedtime snack —

2 large egg whites
⅔ cup sugar
1 cup chocolate chips

Preheat the oven to 325°F. Line 2 cookie sheets with foil and set aside. In a small bowl, beat the egg whites until foamy, gradually add the sugar, and beat on high speed until stiff peaks form. Fold in the chocolate chips and drop the batter by small teaspoonfuls onto the cookie sheets (the cookies should look like small mounds and should not be allowed to spread). Place in the oven, turn off the heat, and let sit overnight.

Note: Also delicious without the chocolate chips, these cookies may be shaped into small nests to hold fruit or flavored whipped cream. They are best stored in an air-tight tin.

Yields 2 dozen

Elizabeth A. Ricker

Pierre Filloeul, French, 1725-1775, *Lady Drinking Tea*, 1725/75, etching, 26 x 31.7 cm. Founders Society Purchase, Hal H. Smith Fund (57.90).

Molasses Cookies

Deliciously spicy —

1 cup shortening
2 cups sugar
½ cup molasses
2 eggs
4 cups flour
4 teaspoons cinnamon
1 teaspoon ginger
1 teaspoon cloves

In a mixing bowl, combine the shortening, sugar, molasses, and eggs and blend thoroughly. Gradually add the dry ingredients, mix well, cover, and chill for several hours or overnight.

Preheat the oven to 350°F. Form the dough into 1-inch balls,* place on a cookie sheet about 2 inches apart, and flatten with a fork. Bake for 8–10 minutes, remove from the oven, and let cool on racks.

*The dough may also be rolled into a log and frozen until ready to use; cut into thin slices and bake as above.

Yields 2 dozen

Beatrice L. Birdsong

Mazurek

Sweet cookies topped with luscious fruit preserves —

1 pound sweet butter
4 cups flour
¾ cup sugar
3 egg yolks
1 whole egg
Strawberry (or other) preserves

In a food processor or with an electric mixer, blend together the butter, flour, sugar, egg yolks, and egg. Cover and chill the dough for a few hours or overnight.

Preheat the oven to 325°F. and grease the bottom and sides of an 11- by 16-inch jelly roll pan. Pat three-quarters of the dough evenly in a layer over the bottom of the pan and spread with the preserves. Roll out the remaining dough to a thickness of ⅛-inch and cut into long strips. Splicing where necessary, place the strips in a criss-cross or lattice pattern diagonally over the preserves. Bake for 1 hour, remove from the oven, and cut into 1½- to 2-inch squares while still warm.

Yields approximately 40

Mrs. Michael J. Bonczak

❧

Crisp Macadamia Wafers

An exotic addition to your favorite assortment —

1 3½-ounce jar macadamia nuts, toasted
¾ cup unsalted butter, softened
½ cup sugar
2 egg whites
½ teaspoon vanilla extract
½ cup flour (approximately)

Preheat the oven to 350°F. Grind enough of the toasted macadamia nuts to measure ½ cup and coarsely chop the remainder; keep the ground and chopped nuts separated and set aside.

Cream the butter until light, add the sugar, beat until fluffy, and stir in the egg whites and vanilla. Transfer the ground nuts to a 1-cup measure and add enough flour to make 1 level cup. Gently stir the flour and nut mixture into the butter mixture, but do not over blend. Drop the dough by small teaspoonfuls 2 or more inches apart on buttered cookie sheets. Dipping in cold water each time, flatten the cookies slightly with the back of a teaspoon. Sprinkle with the chopped nuts and bake for 10 minutes or until the edges of the wafers are browned. Remove at once and cool on racks.

Yields 60

Elsie Golden

Gerry Fischer's Brownies

Chock-full of nuts and marshmallows —

1½ cups butter
6 ounces unsweetened chocolate
4 eggs
2 cups granulated sugar
1 cup flour, sifted
1 cup nuts, chopped
1 teaspoon vanilla
Pinch of salt
Large marshmallows
3 cups confectioner's sugar
¼ cup milk

Preheat the oven to 350°F. In the top of a double boiler, melt together 1 cup of the butter and 4 ounces of the chocolate and set aside to cool. Beat together the eggs and granulated sugar, add the chocolate mixture, beat thoroughly, and mix in the flour, nuts, vanilla, and salt. Pour into a greased 9- by 13-inch pan and bake for 25–30 minutes.

While the brownies are baking, quarter enough marshmallows to cover the top of the brownies completely. As soon as the pan is removed from the oven, place the marshmallows, cut sides down, over the top of the brownies.

In the top of a double boiler, melt the remaining chocolate and butter and 12 of the marshmallows. Add the confectioner's sugar and milk, beat thoroughly, and immediately spread the frosting over the marshmallow-covered brownies. Let stand to cool slightly and refrigerate briefly before cutting.

Yields 12

Vivian Berry

A WASSAIL FEAST

*F*rom its beginning in 1972, the Detroit Institute of Arts' *A Wassail Feast* has attracted nearly 3,000 guests each year. Celebrating the winter holidays in the grand style of the Elizabethan royal court of England, guests form the Grand March and, to the sound of trumpet fanfares, are ushered into the candlelit Great Hall festooned with ribbons and wreaths. Thus begins an unforgettable evening of festival dance and song with a jester, acrobats, a magician, and mimes. There are madrigal singers, strolling minstrels, a Renaissance music ensemble, and a puppeteer — all orchestrated by the Master of Revels. And, of course, there is the feast itself, an experience in lavish dining. Come join in the merrymaking at the next *Wassail Feast*, or prepare these selected recipes for your own holiday celebration! The traditional menu for the *Wassail Feast* features:

Scotch Broth

Prime Roast Beef with Yorkshire Pudding

Roast Capon with Oyster Dressing

Pork and Leek Pie

Sugared Root Vegetables

Flaming Figgy Pudding with Lemon Brandy Sauce

Everflowing Wassail

English, *Punch Pot* (Staffordshire), ca. 1760, ceramic, 18.7 cm. Gift of the Founders Society, The Director's Fund (60.205).

Prime Roast Beef with Yorkshire Pudding

The pride of many a good English tavern —

5–6 pounds sirloin of beef
Black pepper and rosemary to taste
Yorkshire Pudding (recipe follows)
Horseradish sauce (optional)

Preheat the oven to 400°F. Place the beef in a roasting pan, season to taste with the black pepper and rosemary, and place in the oven to roast for about 30 minutes. Reduce the heat to 350° F. and continue roasting at the rate of 20 minutes per pound of beef (plus about 10 minutes) for underdone or 25 minutes to the pound plus 10 minutes for well done. Baste the meat at least three times with the pan juices during roasting. About 30 minutes before the meat is done, place it on the lower shelf of the oven (so that the pudding may be placed on the top shelf). When cooked to the desired doneness, slice the roast and serve with the *Yorkshire Pudding* and horseradish sauce on the side.

Serves 6–8

Yorkshire Pudding

2 eggs, separated
1 cup flour
1 teaspoon olive oil
1 cup milk
Salt and pepper to taste

During the first half-hour that the beef is roasting, prepare the batter for the pudding as follows: In a medium bowl, beat the egg yolks well and gradually add in the flour. Stir in the oil and milk, add salt and pepper to taste, and beat well until the mixture is thick and smooth. Let the batter stand at room temperature until about 30 minutes before the beef is due to be done.

Before baking, stiffly beat the egg whites and blend into the pudding batter. Transfer the batter to a pan containing 1 inch of very hot beef juices — the batter should sizzle as it hits the pan drippings. Place the pudding on the top shelf of the oven and cook during the last 30 minutes of the beef roasting time or until the pudding is golden brown and nicely puffed. Serve at once with the sliced roast beef.

Serves 6–8

Marc Alain Meadows

❧

Roman (Tunisia), *Jug,* ca. 200–300, ceramic, Roman red slip ware, h. 14.3 x diam. 10.5 cm. Founders Society Purchase, Matilda R. Wilson Fund (76.61).

Scotch Broth

Hearty flavor!

1 pound lean lamb stew meat, diced
1–2 tablespoons vegetable oil
1 large onion, chopped
1 large leek (white portion only), sliced
1 turnip, peeled and diced
2 carrots, peeled and diced
2 stalks celery (with leaves), diced
1 medium potato, peeled and diced
½ cup pearl barley, cooked, rinsed, and drained
½ gallon rich lamb, beef, chicken, or vegetable stock
Salt and pepper to taste
Tabasco sauce
2 tablespoons fresh parsley, chopped

In a heavy pot, brown the lamb in the oil, add the onion and leek, and cook over moderate heat until they are a dark golden brown. Add the remaining vegetables, barley, and stock, partially cover the pot, and simmer for 45 minutes or until the meat and barley are tender. Season to taste with salt, pepper, and Tabasco and serve in large bowls sprinkled generously with chopped parsley.

Serves 6–10

The Cookbook Committee

❧

William Burges, English, 1827–1881, *Saint Bacchus Wine and Spirits Sideboard,* (detail) 1858, gilded and painted pine, marble, and iron, 105.4 x 139.1 x 43.2 cm. Gift of Mr. and Mrs. M. E. Cunningham (F82.50).

Pork and Leek Pie

Excellent for large holiday gatherings —

2 leeks, cleaned and sliced
2 medium carrots, peeled and diced
2 stalks celery, diced
2 medium potatoes, peeled and diced
4 cups rich chicken stock
4 tablespoons oil (or 2 tablespoons rendered
  pork fat)
2 pounds lean pork, cut into ½-inch cubes
Salt and pepper to taste
Garlic to taste
1 teaspoon sage
¼ cup flour
Cornstarch combined with cold water
  (optional)
Kitchen Bouquet
Phylo dough

In a large saucepan or kettle, combine the vegetables with a small amount (not more than 1 cup) of the chicken stock and simmer until tender. Drain and reserve the liquid.

In a heavy skillet, heat the oil, brown the pork cubes, and season with salt, pepper, garlic, and sage. Add 2 cups of the stock and braise the pork until tender (30 minutes to 1 hour), letting the liquid evaporate as the pork cooks. Add the flour, stir to make a roux, and cook for 2 minutes. Stir in the remaining chicken stock, add the cooked vegetables and, if the mixture is too thick, add the reserved liquid (if the mixture is too thin, add a little cornstarch dissolved in cold water). Adjust the color with Kitchen Bouquet and seasonings to taste and keep at a simmer over low heat.

Preheat the oven to 350°F. To prepare the top crust, cut 5 pieces of phylo dough* to the outside measurement of one large casserole or 6 individual casseroles (the dough will shrink in baking to fit the inside measurement of the dish). Brush melted butter between the layers of dough and bake until golden brown. Ladle the pork and leek mixture into the casserole(s), cover with the crust(s), and serve.

*Puff pastry or any light, flaky pie dough may be substituted for the phylo.

Note: The pie may be kept warm in a 200°F. oven for up to 15 minutes before serving. If desired, the pork and leek filling may be made in advance and reheated — the crust should be added at the last minute or it may become soggy.

Serves 6

Audley Grossman

Roast Capon with Oyster Dressing

A truly succulent bird —

1 8-pound capon
Salt, pepper, and poultry seasoning to taste
Oyster Dressing (recipe follows)
4 tablespoons butter, softened
1/4 cup butter, melted, combined with 10
    ounces chicken consommé

Preheat the oven to 325° F. Rub the inside of the capon with seasonings to taste, stuff lightly with *Oyster Dressing*, and secure openings with skewers or needle and thread. Rub the outside of the bird with the softened butter, sprinkle with additional seasonings, and place in a roasting pan. Roast the capon uncovered for 2 1/2 hours, basting frequently with the melted butter and consommé mixture, or until the flesh of the bird's thigh is fork-tender.
    Serves 8

Oyster Dressing

2 tablespoons onion, chopped
1/2 cup celery, diced
1/2 cup butter
4 cups white bread, cubed and toasted*
1 teaspoon seasoned salt
1 teaspoon poultry seasoning
1/2 teaspoon pepper
1 egg, beaten slightly
1 cup oysters, chopped

In a large skillet, sauté the onion and celery in the butter, add the bread cubes and seasonings, and stir to blend. Add the egg and the oysters and mix lightly.
    For a cornbread dressing, substitute 2 cups of unsweetened cornbread crumbs for 2 cups of the white bread and decrease the amount of oysters to 1/2 cup.
    Yields sufficient dressing for a 6- to 8-pound bird

The Cookbook Committee

Hubert Gerhard, Dutch, ca. 1540–1620, *Hebe*, ca. 1590, bronze, h. 76 cm. Gift of Mr. and Mrs. Henry Ford II (59.123).

Sugared Root Vegetables

Delicate flavor and smooth texture, an elegant offering —

1 1/2 cups carrots, peeled and diced
1 1/2 cups rutabaga, peeled and diced
1 1/2 cups turnips, peeled and diced
1 1/2 cups parsnips, peeled and diced
3 cups celery root, peeled and diced
1/2 cup butter
2 tablespoons brown sugar
Salt and pepper to taste

Cook each root vegetable separately in boiling water until tender and drain well. Purée each vegetable separately in a food processor or blender — there should be approximately 1 cup of the carrot, rutabaga, turnip, and parsnip purées and 2 cups of the celery root purée. Combine the vegetables in a large saucepan, blend in the butter and brown sugar, and add salt and pepper to taste. Over medium heat, stir the vegetables until heated through and serve.
    Note: This dish freezes well and tastes even better with reheating.
    Serves 6

Bishie Beatty

Flaming Figgy Pudding with Lemon Brandy Sauce

Celebrate the holidays with a touch of drama: turn out the lights, flame this fantastic figgy pudding at tableside, and enjoy the accolades of family and friends.

½ cup fine, dry bread crumbs
1 cup milk, heated
4 eggs, separated
¼ cup sugar
½ pound ground beef suet
¾ cup flour, sifted
1½ teaspoons salt
½ teaspoon mace
⅓ teaspoon cloves
¼ teaspoon cinnamon
½ pound raisins, seeded
2 ounces candied orange peel, chopped
¼ cup figs, chopped finely
2 ounces green citron, chopped
½ cup cider or apple juice, heated to boiling
Brandy
Lemon Brandy Sauce
(recipe follows)

Combine the crumbs and the milk and let stand for 10 minutes. In a large bowl, beat the egg yolks, add the sugar, and beat thoroughly. Blend in the suet and the milk mixture and set aside.

Sift together the flour, salt, and spices, stir in the fruits, and add to the egg yolk mixture. Add the cider and mix well. Beat the egg whites until stiff peaks form and fold into the batter.

Pour the batter into a greased, 2-quart mold, cover, place the mold in a covered pan or on a rack in a Dutch oven, and surround with water to one-half the depth of the mold. Steam the pudding for 3½–4 hours or until springy to the touch, let cool slightly, and unmold.

Soak a length of cheesecloth in the brandy, wrap around the pudding, cover tightly with foil or plastic wrap, and store in the refrigerator for 3 weeks. To serve, warm ⅓–½ cup of brandy, pour over the pudding, and ignite. Slice and serve with *Lemon Brandy Sauce* as soon as the flames have died.
Serves 12–20

Marilyn Gushée

Lemon Brandy Sauce

1 cup sugar
2 tablespoons cornstarch
2 cups boiling water

½ cup butter
Juice of 1 lemon
Rind of 1 lemon, grated
1 tablespoon brandy

In a small saucepan, mix together the sugar and cornstarch and gradually stir in the boiling water. Cook for 5 minutes, remove from the heat, add the butter, and stir until melted. Add the lemon juice, lemon rind, and brandy, stir to blend, and serve hot over *Flaming Figgy Pudding*.
Serves 6–8

The Cookbook Committee

Everflowing Wassail

The more, the merrier!

3 ounces dry sherry
7 12-ounce bottles beer
¼ teaspoon ground nutmeg
½ cup fine, granulated sugar
1 ounce vodka
Spiced, baked apples, sliced
2 lemons, sliced
Cinnamon sticks

In a large pot, combine the sherry, 1 bottle of the beer, the nutmeg, sugar, and vodka and let stand at room temperature for 4 hours. Add the remaining 6 bottles of beer, stirring gently, and serve in large mugs garnished with slices of baked apple and lemon and sticks of cinnamon.
Serves 6–10

The Cookbook Committee

Persian, *Blue-and-white Plate*, 17th cent., Safavid Dynasty, composite body with clear glaze, diam. 45.1 cm. Founders Society Purchase, Mr. and Mrs. Allan Shelden III Fund (82.4).

INDEX

Persian, *Painted Lacquer Binding of a Collection of Prayers in Arabic and Persian,* Qajar Dynasty, 1832, painted lacquer, 20 x 12.2 cm. The Mrs. G. Whitney Hoff Collection, Reference Library (662).

Order Form

A VISUAL FEAST: The Detroit Institute of Arts Cookbook

(please print)	Quantity	Total
Regular price $17.95		$
Founders Society member price $16.15 (10% discount)		
Add 4% Michigan sales tax		
Add $1.50 per book for shipping and handling		
TOTAL		$

Mail to:

Museum Shop, the Detroit Institute of Arts
5200 Woodward Ave., Detroit, MI 48202

Send to:

Name

Address

City   State   Zip

☐ Check enclosed (payable to Founders Society)

☐ American Express   ☐ MasterCard   ☐ Visa

Charge card #   Exp. date

Interbank # (MasterCard only)

Founders Society #

Signature   Phone

Order Form

A VISUAL FEAST: The Detroit Institute of Arts Cookbook

(please print)	Quantity	Total
Regular price $17.95		$
Founders Society member price $16.15 (10% discount)		
Add 4% Michigan sales tax		
Add $1.50 per book for shipping and handling		
TOTAL		$

Mail to:

Museum Shop, the Detroit Institute of Arts
5200 Woodward Ave., Detroit, MI 48202

Send to:

Name

Address

City   State   Zip

☐ Check enclosed (payable to Founders Society)

☐ American Express   ☐ MasterCard   ☐ Visa

Charge card #   Exp. date

Interbank # (MasterCard only)

Founders Society #

Signature   Phone